David Ward
Bay of Hope
Five Years in
Newfoundland

Published in Canada by ECW Press
665 Gerrard Street East
Toronto, Ontario, Canada M4M 1Y2
416-694-3348 / info@ecwpress.com

Editor: Michael Holmes
Cover design: David A. Gee
Author photo: Robin Barriball

LIBRARY AND ARCHIVES CANADA
CATALOGUING IN PUBLICATION

Ward, David, 1958–, author
Bay of hope : five years in Newfoundland /
David Ward.

Includes bibliographical references.
Issued in print and electronic formats.
ISBN 978-1-77041-382-5 (softcover).
ALSO ISSUED AS: 978-1-77305-162-8 (PDF),
978-1-77305-161-1 (EPUB)

1. Ward, David, 1958–.
2. Ecologists—Newfoundland and Labrador—
Biography. 3. Adventure and adventurers—
Newfoundland and Labrador—Biography.
4. Loneliness. 5. Solitude. 6. Autobiographies.

I. TITLE.

QH31.W37A3 2018   577.092
C2017-906597-1   C2017-906598-X

The publication of *Bay of Hope* has been generously supported by the Canada Council for the Arts
which last year invested $153 million to bring the arts to Canadians throughout the country, and by the
Government of Canada through the Canada Book Fund. *Nous remercions le Conseil des arts du Canada
de son soutien. L'an dernier, le Conseil a investi 153 millions de dollars pour mettre de l'art dans la vie des
Canadiennes et des Canadiens de tout le pays. Ce livre est financé en partie par le gouvernement du Canada.*
We also acknowledge the Ontario Arts Council (OAC), an agency of the Government of Ontario, and
the contribution of the Government of Ontario through the Ontario Book Publishing Tax Credit and
the Ontario Media Development Corporation.

PRINTED AND BOUND IN CANADA

PRINTING: MARQUIS   5   4   3   2   1

for my sister, Wendy

(1952–1979)

Part One

one

Newfoundland and Labrador will dramatically increase spending to encourage residents of some isolated communities to move to larger towns. Finance Minister Jerome Kennedy said government will offer as much as $270,000 for each household to relocate.

— *CBC News*, March 26, 2013

Do you realize you can buy an oceanfront house in Newfoundland for $10,000? Perched on granite cliffs rising several hundred feet in the air. In a small working fishing village equipped with high speed-internet, a store, a school, a medical centre, a community hall, a ferry service, a bed and breakfast, and a church. With a surprisingly moderate winter climate and a pace of life unlike any you probably know. Where whales break the ocean's surface a short distance from your front door while bald eagles soar overhead.

And where, on a nice day, you can see France — St. Pierre et Miquelon — as you stroll the boardwalk.

Your neighbours will be kind, generous, hard-working people capable of providing you with guidance, physical support, and food products of the land and sea. And if you do settle, your new-found friends won't want you to fail. They don't say so directly but their actions speak loudly. They conclude that you are low on firewood and in various ways work collectively to see that you have enough to get through winter. Or for no apparent reason they hand you a loaf of homemade bread and a fresh-caught cod.

I'm talking about an isolated outport called McCallum. Please don't see my thoughts as an effort to sell you something — this is just an FYI from an excitable guy. For five years, iconic Canadian authors Claire and Farley Mowat called Newfoundland's Southwest Coast home. Fifty years later, I'm thrilled to say the same.

Last home on the right, I tell visitors when they ask where my house can be found. But even I don't find my home that easy to get to. Just getting off the ferry is tricky for me. I know it is second nature for my neighbours, but I'm terrible at it. While passing parcels off and onboard, I'm scared I'll slip between the boat and the bumpers. Anybody who's seen me do this work can tell I'm terrified at low tide.

Wherever I am on the wharf, I need to remind myself that that ferry carries cargo that requires craning. The safest choice I can make is to wave a quick goodbye to the boys on the boat, say hello to friends awaiting freight, and get my big butt out of harm's way.

As I walk away from the wharf, I consider how long it will be before I touch land again. That's a surprising characteristic about McCallum's boardwalk — it's built so solid, with buildings on both sides, I'm convinced I'm on land. But it actually runs a lengthy distance over water, past a fisheries facility, a house, a store, a post office, and several sheds before it finally arrives at a hill. But what a hill it hits. Up and down. I grab the rail and dig into the cleats, all the while carrying whatever goods I'm bringing back. I sneak a peek at Matt Fudge's unintentionally aesthetically stacked firewood and glance to see if anyone is coming down the steep road to my right. McCallum calls its boardwalks roads, but there are no cars in McCallum. Neither the rugged terrain nor the provincially funded ferry can accommodate cars.

I look to see if the men lazing around the slip are trying to tease me, and I listen to hear if any of the women hanging laundry wants to talk. Then I turn left. Going right would take me to some fun places — to dear friends, the community hall, McCallum's school, or a hike on the hill — but that route heads away from my house. So it's past a dog that hates me, several hip-roofed homes, colourful sheds, a low-slung bed-and-breakfast building, piled lobster pots, some beautiful hand-built boats, and yards full of fun folk art, all nicely located before a backdrop of granite and green. Then the boardwalk weaves out over the water again, where everything smells of brine. It's up another steep bridge and around a curvy corner before I get a glimpse of my home sitting high on the hill. It might not be the biggest house, or the cutest, or the best cared for, but it's mine and I love it.

Getting goods to my house can be challenging. Like the day my new washer, dryer, fridge, stove, and freezer arrived on the ferry. If not for the help of friends, those appliances would still be sitting on the wharf. Because nothing makes its way across McCallum without significant support. Just ask tourists Richard and Ann Brenton who, upon their ferry's arrival in McCallum, are greeted by Herman Fudge, who, because the Brentons showed up carrying backpacks, determines he needs to direct our visitors to a clearing where they can camp. Herman's intense style of communication reminds me of the role Dustin Hoffman played as Tom Cruise's brother in the Oscar-winning movie *Rain Man*.

"Where you from?" the thickset, wide-eyed forty-six-year-old asks the Kootenay, B.C., couple before moving on to questions about their favourite hockey team. After making sure the Brentons know he is a Leafs fan, Herman pushes his cap a little higher on his head and repeats, "British Columbia?" like he didn't quite catch it the first time, and then, "I got a sister in Calgary. Angela. Her daughter's Olivia. Olivia's my niece. Cute little Olivia. And husband Darryl from Spaniard's Bay, Newfoundland. Yes sir, Newfoundland! They are coming home for the Fudge reunion. Oh my God, it's July already. Can you believe it? Darts will be starting soon. I'm looking forward to that. Darts are good fun. Do you play darts?"

It's because of his commitment to his unofficial job as McCallum's greeter that Herman has gotten to know all who come and go in this outport — more than thirty years of ferry employees, utility workers, vacationers, sailors, artists, plant personnel, politicians, fish farmers, government staff, transient teachers . . . It is because of Herman's efforts to be such a sociable soul that he makes friends of almost every visitor. It's also why he receives so many Christmas cards.

"Yes, he does, my dear," says Herman's eloquent Aunt Sarah, who, in addition to providing Herman with huge love, supports him in all Christmas-card-related activities, keeping track of incoming and changing addresses, seeing that he sends as many as he receives, and managing his budget. "It's not a big deal," the mother of seven stoically insists, "but it does take a little care. We update our records first thing in the new year, and then around November we look at it all again. Cards come from new people right up until December 24, so we try to reply to those right away. That way Herman's newest friends don't have to wait a year to hear from him."

"The Christmas card that comes the farthest is the one from Ireland," Sarah says. "And the other day he got a post-card from Denmark. But not counting all the birthday cards he gets, and the one St. Patrick's Day card that his cousin Sandra sends him from St. John's, Herman got eighty-eight cards last Christmas. Because whether you are a stranger who only stays in McCallum for a few minutes or one of many who moved away forever, no one forgets who Herman is."

No one fails to remember McCallum either. While there are other places in Canada where you can find com-munities that are distinctly different from what you're accustomed to, they're nowhere near the forty-ninth par-allel like McCallum is. Even most Newfoundlanders don't know what life is like here. It's like Greece, only in Canada. I don't mean it's exactly like Greece, but that it's a foreign feeling to find yourself experiencing someplace so dramat-ically different while still standing on Canadian soil. Even locals who have never known otherwise find it impossible to take McCallum's remarkableness for granted. "There is very little like McCallum, my son," even the most cynical will say. "And I don't believe there are many places like Newfoundland's Sou'west Coast."

The Southwest's absence of automobiles is noticeable. I've seen mainlanders go quiet for days in response to McCallum's zero-car qualities. The thought that, in the event of an emergency, you're a three-hour boat ride from a waiting ambulance can paralyze even the bravest of travellers. Especially when rough seas do away with your options entirely. Just using a sharp knife to cut carrots on a cutting board makes visitors consider the ferry schedule, recall the forecast, and proceed with caution — something the locals would laugh at, if such a thought actually occurred to them.

Employment doesn't dominate McCallum life either. No Newfoundlander has ever asked me what I do for a living, yet I can't go a week in Ontario without answering that inquiry. It's like there is some kind of comparison game going on in Ontario, and everybody is playing.

Imagine the discomfort Ontarians experience when I tell them that I quit a full-time college faculty position, four years short of early retirement, to go live in an isolated Newfoundland outport. When I present that news publicly, many in the audience respond with an impulsive groan followed by an uncontrollable giggle, indicating that they're largely unsure and a little bit rude. Then they quickly whisper, "He must have money," and that renders them wrong — I gave what little I had to an investor at the time and have been living like I've got nothing ever since.

Anyone who's ever been part of institutional life knows I had good reason for leaving. Such organizations are toxic, and their self-serving leadership lethal. Yet many people can't cope with the thought that I gave up more than $1 million in earnings over the final nine years of my work life to move to McCallum to write. They can't comprehend the idea that I might be as passionate about studying the human condition as they are about making money. They only show signs of overcoming their discomfort with my choices when I tell them that I continue to teach a course online — like that $13,000 a year puts me on easy street.

Then I really mess with their heads — I drop the news regarding resettlement. I tell them how I've been offered $250,000 to leave McCallum, showing that the more I try to *not* make money, the more that money follows me around. This thought too is alien to Ontarians, as is their likelihood of ever leaving the tribe.

I remember walking along King Street in Toronto. I had agreed to be interviewed for a satellite radio show about a book I'd written on what it feels like for a fifty-year-old man to go in search of his childhood hero and find him. I wanted to arrive at the radio station early, so I gave myself lots of time to look around. I saw many others on that route as well. Thousands. But they weren't watching me. They were staring at their phones while they walked to work. It started as soon as I left my hotel room, when the woman waiting in front of me, with her face buried deep in her phone, didn't realize our elevator had arrived. It was only when I pushed past her to hold back that elevator's quickly closing doors that she waddled in, her thumbs moving at a million miles per hour.

The same thing occurred as I dodged bodies along King. I saw people everywhere, walking with their heads down and their shoulders sloped, all giving their phones a good fingering. They looked like actors in an unsettling science fiction movie — one where everyone has been programmed to walk hunched over, following whatever instructions they're receiving through a handheld device they're holding in a prayer-like fashion in front of them.

It reminds me of a conversation I had with an outport person in Little Bay Islands, another isolated Newfoundland community that's been offered resettlement money. That lobster fisherman told me that he had been to Toronto and found it difficult to get directions because no one wanted to help him. He said he stood at Bay and Dundas feeling more lost than if you had dropped him blindfolded in the wilds of Labrador. "And understand this," he adamantly added. "My wife died in a car crash, so I know what it's like to be lonely. But I never felt so alone in my life as I did that day when I got lost in one of the most populated parts of Ontario . . . No sir — I never felt so alone in my life."

two

The issue of resettlement has been politically charged in Newfoundland and Labrador for generations, particularly since a government-led program that peaked in the 1950s and 1960s.

Yet the governing Tories have said they have been feeling the strain of providing standards of government services to rural communities, even though the province's population has been becoming increasingly urban.

— *CBC News*, March 26, 2013

Born David William Ward in Kitchener, Ontario, September 13, 1958, I grew up the middle child of five but the only son for thirteen years. As the only boy in that era, I had privileges that my sisters didn't. They had to look after me, do household chores, get good grades, and frequently feed me, while I pretty much did what I pleased — a pattern that, while it convinced me I was worthy, came with its share of shortcomings. Like a lack of domestic lessons learned and a loss of considerable confidence as a result — a situation that

I spent the first twenty-five years of my adult life attempting to overcome, with direction from a world of women all too willing to provide opinions.

With an alcoholic father and an egomaniac mother, my ride wasn't all fun and games. But, to be fair, my father was a good provider, and, as a young woman, my mother wanted nothing more than to raise a family. In defense of my dad, he didn't drink for the first twenty-one years of my life. My father went back to drinking when his oldest daughter and son-in-law died in an automobile crash. With a convincing reason to go back to the booze, Dad went on a ten-year binge that made life miserable for Mom and my little brother, who was only eight at the time of the tragedy. The rest of us, all young adults, bailed. I can't imagine what life looked like to my mother who, at forty-nine, faced a drunk, a dead daughter and son-in-law, a decade of depression, and a young child to care for.

After backpacking Australia for a year, I attended university where I met and married Janet, and the two of us spent the next eleven years discovering new ways to hurt each other. We should have been great together, but we were unbelievably naive. Fortunately, when the marriage ended, we had no children. Yet, as a result of not having kids, Janet and I have not had reason to see each other since, and I, for one, find this unfortunate.

Janet was stunning. I use the past tense to describe Janet's beauty because she's no longer mine, and I haven't seen her for twenty years. But I don't doubt she has aged gracefully. She always took care of herself and she's got great genes — her mother and her sisters are also striking. And Janet was clever. Smart as smart can be. She was a tall, slender, doe-eyed accountant. I bet if *I* had been smarter — in a relationship-related way — we might have survived as a unit. Instead we were young and stupid.

I think about Janet every day. We had considerable commonality regarding what we thought was sweet, and we cared in similar ways, about the less fortunate and family. We also had some similarity in the way we felt about money — we knew we needed it, but we did not see it as significant regarding our overall happiness.

I remember the outstanding job Janet did of making our less-than-adequate living environments homey. She was creative. To this day, my most prized possession — the one item I'd grab in the event of a fire — is a stained glass business card holder that Janet made me. I don't use business cards anymore, but I see that cardholder as a beautiful piece of art, and the most precious article I own. I've kept it safe through three challenging moves over thousands of kilometres.

I loved Janet's family. Not that I found feeling anything easy, especially given the difficulties Janet and I faced daily just trying not to unload unresolved anger on each other. But Janet's family was good to me. So I've got some regrets.

After Janet came Carol — another beauty. Not the kind of beauty that morally deficient magazine covers call for. More of a natural gorgeousness, with an ageless complexion and a captivating cuteness. Carol arrived in my life at the perfect time, bringing to my forties something special that supported the considerable personal and professional growth I invested deeply in during that decade.

Carol taught psychology, an area of expertise I was excited to explore. Plus, Carol didn't want to marry or live together — a choice I supported. We'd both been through that: she had two grown-up sons and was enjoying her freedom, and I no longer wanted anyone to witness my bad habits on a daily basis. So we talked extensively on the phone and came together on weekends and holidays, giving each other at least twenty-four hours of intense attention before returning to our respective workweeks.

A busty, blond, understated sexpot, Carol was a dream on many levels, but her family history was not helpful.

I'm convinced that Carol's late mother, who was born to McCallum folks who had moved to Halifax, learned some bad parenting practices from *her* mom. So Carol's a huge success story. That she came out of that confusion to achieve work success, accumulate wealth, and raise two fine boys is nothing short of amazing. But when the baggage she brought along for the ride collided with my own substantial suitcases, it was the cause of our demise.

Carol and I were a partnership for a dozen years, most of which were wonderful. But, in the end, that train too came off the tracks, eventually freeing me up to flee Ontario. Yet again I fell hard. Five years have passed and I'm still not entirely over her. It's been additionally difficult trying to heal in McCallum because finding this community was a result of following Carol's roots. Carol has twelve blood relatives in this tiny town, and this building I now call home is Carol's house too. We initially bought it as a summer residence, together. It's still full of her stuff — belongings that I believe will never leave this community because getting Carol to McCallum always required a large physical and emotional effort from me.

Carol's McCallum connection has only gotten harder for her. Everyone knew her and liked her here, and several occasionally miss her, enough that they often ask about her.

They want to know if I think she'll ever visit McCallum again, and I truthfully tell them that I don't believe she will. But I always make sure they know that Carol loved McCallum.

So I've got no regrets regarding my relationship with Carol. Many matters do get better with age if an adult really wants them to. Some things truly improve when you learn to make smarter, kinder choices and open yourself up to new information, as I did regarding my connection with Carol. It turns out that, after admitting to a long list of personal imperfections, I am comfortable saying that I didn't do a bad job of loving Carol.

Yet I still find the agony that comes with the ending of an intimate relationship excruciating. If I thought it would work, I'd forfeit something of tremendous value to take away the torture at the time. The best I can do is remind myself that the pain will eventually lessen. Yes, we all know those who quickly find themselves a new honey. People who, when I ask them how they're doing — three months after splitting up — tell me that they're over it. I know others who say the answer lies in getting drunk and laid as often as they can, but immediately jumping back into the blaze and self-medicating has never worked for me. The only thing that works for me is to soberly stare down the monster

— the ogre being the anger that I'm experiencing in response to the hurt and fear I'm feeling.

Not that a person can't heal in the company of another. Just that I need to think my sorrow through, over and over and often alone, until I recognize the source of my sadness. I have to find ways to move that circle of hurt into a more truthful, healthy place, and that process takes time. The two-year mark barely lifts a large cloud for me. I have little disposition for denial, and I hate the blaming game. Self-deception only results in further painful, brain-bound data looping farther from the truth, until I eventually have to deal with it on some heartfelt level of self-honesty if I'm to have any chance at all of moving on. Or if I'm to have any hope whatsoever of being able to answer questions like: What now, after concluding that I ache for the intimacy of another? How does that affect what my current life looks like, what with no eligible women living in McCallum? And, even if single women did visit this outport (a few do every summer), what are the odds that I could make a good connection with one of them?

Just *meeting* women in McCallum is a challenge. I guess I could ask Nina Crant — the missus who manages McCallum's bed and breakfast — to let me know when an unattached woman arrives, alerting me to pay attention for such a sight and to make sure I've shaved and showered before leaving home. But that kind of proactive effort requires I go public in my pursuit of a partner — a concept I'm not comfortable with in a town this tiny, because a small community can be an emotionally unsafe place to explore intimacy and experience pain when everybody's got a front row seat. Plus, planning makes me feel like I'm pushing, rather than allowing for something organic to grow. I don't want just anyone, of course. And that bed and breakfast sees less than seventy visitors per year, with those guests mostly being couples, male hydro workers, or seniors in search of their roots. The number of available women who visit McCallum is miniscule.

I've also concluded that if I have any chance of making a meaningful connection of a romantic sort, that woman will likely come from Canada's mainland because when speaking with women from away, they often say, "I can see what you like about this lifestyle." But when a Newfoundland woman realizes McCallum is my year-round residence, she'll most commonly inquire, "Why would you live in McCallum when you could be on a road where you can drive to a mall?"

That's why online dating makes so much sense — it increases your chances, choices, and reach. Yet not everyone finds online dating to their liking. Many find it scary.

I think internet dating is less frightening than the way adults dated over the previous fifty years, somehow depending on stumbling across compatible people in similar circumstances, in bars or at work. Online, you get a considerable-sized selection of people to pick from, all of whom, by being there, are admitting they are open to the discussion and, in many cases, have declared what they're after — dating, a relationship, or sex. Nobody is required to provide his or her real name or actual address, and everyone is welcome to proceed at whatever pace works for them. All from the safety and comfort of their computers, a place that has the potential to open up a planet full of possibilities.

I think something that stops a lot of wannabe daters in isolated areas from online exploration is a certainty that no one wants to move to a far-off community — an opinion that I don't share. While I may be the only mainlander who has made McCallum my home, I can't be the only individual who might consider the idea. But because so many Newfoundlanders surrender to the city, those who remain rural expect that no one from away will ever want to share a life with them. But that's just not true. There is a movement among many mainlanders to find a kinder, gentler way of life than the one they've been living. It's obvious to these seekers of a sustainable lifestyle that today's younger generation is the first that will not live a better quality of life than those who came before them. This junior group is no longer sucked into believing the bullshit that their parents, big business, and government give them and is looking elsewhere for answers — including rural Newfoundland.

I also think that people in isolated areas avoid internet dating because of the loss of privacy that occurs when online participants eventually hook up. Yet I don't believe anyone in search of love should rule out exploring online. They simply need to go into such circumstances knowing that it might take considerable time, energy, and courage before connecting with someone who values them and their home. And that they might make mistakes in the meantime. But the technology is not the problem — it's hurtful and hurt-filled people who make dating difficult, and that's nothing new.

three

According to the Department of Municipal Affairs, a single person owning a house in a community where 90 percent of the residents vote to move will receive $250,000; a couple with no dependents will receive $260,000 while a family of three or more will get $270,000. Of course we will respect whatever decision people in the smaller communities make if it comes down to a vote on relocation. However, it could be a good time to take the money and run, before government officials change their minds about the funding announced in the budget.

— Clayton Hunt, *The Coast of Bays Coaster*, April 11, 2013

Even when you love it like I do, McCallum life isn't easy. To know that McCallum is an isolated outport is one thing. To know that McCallum's nearest neighbours on both sides are also isolated outports and that the closest of those is on an island twenty-two kilometres away is something else entirely. McCallum is an isolated outport among isolated outports, making it a long way away from *everything*.

The Newfoundland region that encompasses these remote communities is called the Southwest Coast. Few contest where the Southwest Coast begins in the west — Channel-Port aux Basques — but where to assign the Southwest's official starting point in the east is arguable. Meteorological experts see the Southwest as beginning at the bottom of the Burin Peninsula. Yet such separation leaves a large piece of Placentia Bay without definite identification. So I've concluded that the eastern locus of the Southwest Coast is Fortune Bay's Grand le Pierre and that the Burin Peninsula is an environment all on its own.

My *symbolic* Southwest, however — the area that represents *my* Newfoundland — starts at Hermitage Cove in the east and extends to the archipelago of Burgeo in the west, a distance of 163 kilometres unless you're actually following the ragged coastline of capes, fiords, and headlands, in which case you can quintuple the distance. This is the territory that I explore at every opportunity. This is where the boats that I access travel to — other isolated communities like Francois, Ramea, and Gaultois. And Grey River, home to 123 hardy outport people.

Grey River is often criticized and bullied from afar, by come-from-aways and locals alike. The community's basic way of life makes them an easy target for those who need to see themselves as superior, yet I find Grey River refreshing. Despite experiencing harsh pressures — economic and otherwise — Grey River is resisting resettlement more than most.

While Grey River has several times suffered some serious heartache, its citizens seldom resent living the isolated life. That makes them a minority in this day and age, when complaining is so common. Grey River is also unusually answerable regarding their grief. Check out the monument they've recently plunked down in the middle of town:

In loving memory of Harriet and Caroline Young, age 12 years, died December 21, 1913, twin daughters of Frank and Annie Young, and niece Mary Lushman who died at 16 years. We shall meet again.

"Yes, my dear. But there is more to those deaths than what you see on that gravestone," a delicate Sarah Rose, age eighty-one, tells me after I am introduced to her by the kind young couple who manage Grey River's general store.

"But if you want more," Sarah insists, gently touching my arm, "you will need to come to my house where I have a picture of those three little darlings before they died." So it's off to Sarah's home I go.

"Tom Young sent this picture to my [late] husband, Victor, because poor old Victor's mother died when he was only eleven months. He didn't know what she looked like," Sarah says, pointing to a young girl in a surprisingly high-quality photograph of a large group of Grey River children, circa 1913. "Eleven months is not a long time to have your mother's love," she adds. "Today they might know what Victor's mother died from [mastitis, maybe], but back then they didn't.

"And here," Sarah notes, circling three more lovely female faces, "are Mary, Caroline, and Harriet — the little girls who died when their house burned down. Nobody knows how the fire started, but the girls' mother was a midwife who had gone to help another daughter [also named Annie] have a baby. The girls' father was up the bay. So the only one at home with the girls was a teacher who was boarding, and he jumped out the window when he saw the house was on fire.

"A week later, the daughter that the mother was helping have a baby, and the baby, died [of childbirth complications, apparently, both of them]. So the older Annie lost three daughters, a niece she raised as one of her own, and a grand-child, all in one week. The poor old woman was never the same. She didn't know what she was at. She'd put out plates on the table and sing out, 'Caroline, Mary, Harriet — come for dinner.' Of course they never come. Poor thing just got out of it. Can hardly blame her," says Sarah, a mother of ten, clearly touched by her own storytelling.

"So their people bought them that gravestone and put it where their house was at. But that's all I know," she concludes, trying to bring closure to what was clearly a tough story to tell. "But maybe I'm wrong, because I wasn't born in 1913. So if you need more, you will want to get it from somebody else. You see, what I tell you, I got from my mother, but she's been dead thirty-six years. Maybe my mother was wrong, but I don't think so — Mother had too good a memory to make mistakes on things like that. No, my dear, my mother had too good a memory to make mistakes about one of the Sou'west's saddest stories. I think if somebody has made mistakes here, it's me."

If I had to move from McCallum, it would be to Grey River. I respect their resilience.

Writers Claire and Farley Mowat lived a large part of the 1960s on Newfoundland's Southwest Coast. Sailing their thirty-six-foot sloop, *Happy Adventure*, from Hermitage Bay to Burgeo, the Mowats identified earlier than anyone the eventual death of the outports. Documenting their observations in books like *Bay of Spirits*, *This Rock within the Sea*, and *The Outport People*, this adventurous couple provided an up-close look at what life was like alongside Newfoundland's granite wall after the island's 1949 commitment to Canada.

Bay of Spirits is a love story. Experiencing small but once relevant communities that have since resettled, the Mowats ponder a time when the two of them explored every cleft and cranny of not only each other, but the far-reaching fiord that locals call Bay Despair — "Bay Despair" being a bastardization of the cartographically correct name, Bay d'Espoir, which ironically means Bay of Hope. (But it bears noting that, long before either name came across the pond, natives called this incredible inlet Bay of Spirits; Farley was the first to foster this fact.)

With *This Rock within the Sea*, Farley recorded what he knew was a vanishing way of life. And, while many believe Claire's *Outport People* to be a journal of her and Farley's five years in Burgeo, I see it as more of a description of the island's internal conflict and contrasting customs — documentation I dearly need when I have difficulty understanding the differences between where I come from and where I am today.

It was the provocative pictures of a spectacular fair-haired Claire taken almost fifty years ago that the couple included in *Bay of Spirits* that prompted me to phone Mrs. Mowat — prior to her husband's passing — at their home in River Bourgeois, Cape Breton. I said I wanted to speak with the author about her book, but I really wished for some kind of connection with a come-from-away woman who had also experienced this lovely locale. Which Claire was pleased to provide. "I'm thrilled to hear that people are still in places like McCallum," she said. "I mean, Farley and I were worried for them when their cod fishery collapsed [in 1992]. We were genuinely concerned that that would be it for the outport way of life. So to hear from you that there are still communities holding on along that lovely seacoast and among those beautiful mountains is great news.

"Newfoundland was such a special place for me to begin my life with Farley. It was amazing to live somewhere that was so much more sound and sane than what I'd grown up with in Toronto, where there is such a pressure to prove yourself as better than others. Not that Newfoundland didn't have some of that too, but most of the outport people didn't feel they had to flaunt it, to humiliate others. All this was, for me, a wonderful window on human nature.

"So to hear from you that their lives are more comfortable

than they were when Farley and I were there, that they've acquired more of life's conveniences, like a daily ferry and regular visits from nurses and doctors, is good news. Farley and I are glad for them for that. But mostly, after all these years, we're pleased to hear that there are still people on Newfoundland's Sou'west Coast who are still living remarkable lives."

Burgeo is not as kind as Claire. Burgeo residents insist on finding fault with Farley. Few have read his work, and none admit to having a problem with him personally, yet they all say they know someone who does. So let's set something straight — I'm a fan of both parties, and while I've got buddies in Burgeo, I never met or spoke with Mr. Mowat. I have always liked Farley's literary efforts, and I especially enjoy his Newfoundland narratives. Farley loved Newfoundlanders. And because I also admire folks who for hundreds of years stared down danger, I respect Burgeo's past. But these two strong-willed seafarers have not been friends since 1967, when Farley reported to the world an incident in which Burgeo residents mercilessly killed a landlocked whale.

So where do I stand regarding Burgeo and Farley's fifty-year fight? I believe both participants were right, and wrong. I trust Mowat reported what he witnessed, and that what he witnessed was ugly. But Burgeo residents didn't want to hear about it, nor did they want anyone else to be aware of their embarrassing behaviour. To which I say, too bad — adults are accountable for their actions.

I also believe that outport people of that era had a relationship with nature that was more instinctive than caring. More like a domestic cat that's uncaringly cornered a mouse in the kitchen. I forgive them for that — a possibility that Farley could have considered. Plus, I wonder what would have happened to that whale had it been allowed to live in such a contained environment — something that balanced reporting could have helped to conclude.

But Burgeo residents had nearly five decades to grow up regarding their grudges. And for that entire time, they failed to act in a mature way. I think the people of Burgeo should have shown the nonagenarian Mowat that they meant him no harm. Because, in *Bay of Spirits*, Farley said some insensitive things about my McCallum. Yet when I let go of my own irritation regarding Farley's callous analysis and I read between the lines, I begin to believe that he trusted some selfish, insecure sources and that he also gave an accurate assessment of a community experiencing suffocating control at the hands of an influential merchant — a trader who had the power to set a low price for outgoing fish products and charge a high cost for incoming goods.

I've concluded that, despite Farley's rudeness regarding McCallum people and the state of their homes in the sixties, McCallum residents value him for what he was — a courageous communicator who came to comment on the Southwest Coast when most Canadians couldn't have cared less. "Farley said our homes looked slovenly," McCallum's proudest fisherman, Tim Fudge, says, "and I don't doubt they did." So I think it's a shame that Burgeo wasted all those years when they could have wished Farley safe sailing. Yet it's revealing to see that, despite screwing up so badly regarding that innocent whale and bringing so much negative attention to Newfoundland's Southwest Coast, Burgeo has, for fifty years, clung to their anger like it's a lifesaver, rather than the killer it actually is.

four

An official with the provincial government's Department of Municipal Affairs will be in McCallum in late August to hold an information session about possible resettlement. Apparently, a recent unofficial poll in McCallum resulted in 79 percent of eligible residents voting for resettlement.

— *The St. John's Telegram*, August 2, 2013

I wish the town of McCallum had kept its name Bonne Bay. It was changed to honour the Newfoundland governor shortly after the time of his term. Bonne Bay is a poetic title and fitting tribute to the Southwest Coast's French history, and it's semantically correct given that "bonne" means "good." The only pleasure I get from knowing this outport was named after a British colonizer comes from learning that Sir Henry Edward McCallum didn't get along with politicians, including Newfoundland premier Robert Bond, the son of a St. John's merchant. That's why Henry served such a short time as governor of Newfoundland (1899–1901) before being appointed elsewhere, because of the tension between the two men.

Henry's fast transfer out of Newfoundland was unfortunate, given that every region Henry governed — except Newfoundland — grew immensely. Henry McCallum was a huge success. It appears that Newfoundland's failure to grow as much as Henry's other colonies — Lagos, Natal, Ceylon — is a direct result of government's long-term mismanagement of the island's fishery and extended economy, because Newfoundlanders gave birth to a comparable number of children, but with there being no work, Newfoundlanders were forced to assemble their families elsewhere. All of which makes me wonder: If government post–Henry McCallum had been competent, how many people would reside in Newfoundland now? And how many would live in McCallum, a community that, while its population peaked at 284 in the late 1980s, has the same number of residents today — 79 — as it did when Henry was governor?

It's easy to see why rural Newfoundland is dying. Children grow up and leave for work or school and don't come back, while the rest of us just get older. You don't have to be a mathematician to figure out what happens next.

What I don't understand is why so many people from else-where feel compelled to tell McCallum residents that their hometown is at death's door. I write for a Newfoundland newspaper — I'm trying to live *The Shipping News* dream — so, via email, snail mail, social media, and site visits, I meet a lot of people, many of whom insist on telling me that the outports are dying. But, never mind me, nobody is on the receiving end of this unwanted information more than McCallum residents, who habitually hear it from friends, family, and others who have moved away. Like the inhab-itants hadn't noticed. I suspect this need for the informer to feel smart at the expense of others is similar to what fol-lowers of professional wrestling face when non-fans insist on telling fans, "It's fake, you know?" No kidding? Or, as they say in Newfoundland: "The devil?"

Scroll through Newfoundland newspapers online. Whenever an article appears containing content about an isolated outport, a lot of readers post heated comments implying that every outport person deserves to rot in hell for finding themselves in a situation where government has offered them a buyout. It's unsettling to think that so many of this angry gang are out there, holding on so tightly to their badly informed beliefs. These ignorant individuals, behind anonymous names like "God Bless Britain" and "u don tno," see themselves as having a keen understanding of Canada's most complex socioeconomic issues.

The groups that represents these haters — their governments — are not a lot different. The only difference is that, for governments, silence is the tool of choice because not standing up for rural populations ruffles the fewest feathers — a significant part of any government goal.

I suspect that most politicians are too full of fear to act otherwise. I'm sure some of them went into service with the best intentions, but, once within their power-worshiping parties, they find themselves neutered by pompous blowhards who use intimidating tactics like humiliation to keep their doubters at bay. Otherwise, how did Premier Danny Williams consistently get away with placing smiling, clapping women — like McCallum's member of the house of assembly — behind him whenever the camera was on, in an effort to capture the female vote and the male viewer? Why would any self-respecting woman agree to such lapdog duties unless she felt she had no choice? So, while this pitiable group of politicians may not have the same desire that their voters do to repeatedly point out to outport people their eventual expiry, they do make daily decisions, behind closed doors, that contribute to the death of rural Newfoundland.

Consider the predicament faced by McCallum's adorable

charmer Sidney Simms. Sid has leukemia. He's been battling this horrible disease for seven years, but when I try to talk with him about it, he just gives me a big smile and giggles, "Beautiful day, isn't it?" And then, in classic Newfoundland fashion, he partially repeats himself: "Yes sir — beautiful day."

I'm not sure why Sidney won't share more. Maybe he believes that talking about his illness will interfere with his efforts to live life to its fullest. Or maybe it's a point of accomplishment — few of us ever courageously confront the face of death and stare it down as successfully as Sidney does. So perhaps Sid has decided he doesn't want to talk about his war with cancer with someone who hasn't experienced such sickness.

I don't blame Sidney if he sees me as unworthy of his hard-earned wisdom or if he thinks it's none of my business. I also wouldn't condemn him if he was scared, but I don't believe that fear is the cause of Sidney's silence. I think he's full of stubborn pride. He's the last guy who would want to believe he was better than anyone else, in need of sympathy or wanting for anything other than a day of good weather. Because Sidney and his partner, Olive, are full-time fishers. Up before dawn in an effort to bring in their bounty, these two strong souls look for little more from life than occasional time with their out-of-town kids.

But I hear that Sidney's leukemia is kicking up again — that he's going to have to get tested for it more frequently. Nothing too demanding or costly at this point in time, I'm told. Nothing that should keep him from sleeping in his own bed or so far from home that he can't scratch out a living, as long as the province of Newfoundland and Labrador and a few of its ratepayers are agreeable to making some minor changes to McCallum's ferry schedule.

"Fat chance that'll happen," my officemate used to say, during the part of my life when I was paid by the province of Ontario.

"It's better for one voter to die than to allow another to get pissed off at the party," the politically sensitive professor preached. "Especially during an election year."

As for the flexibility of ferry users, I believe that those with the most are often so full of fear that they can't consider giving up even the tiniest bit of what they grasp onto. That's why the most contemptuous relationship on the Southwest Coast is between two towns — McCallum and its nearest neighbour, Gaultois. The battlefield on which that war is waged is the *Terra Nova* — the fifty-year-old former hydrographic vessel that connects the communities with goods and services.

The *Terra Nova* is the lifeline that gives Gaultois three

times more service than it does McCallum. Yet Gaultois argues McCallum should get *no* assistance from the *Terra Nova* — a claim that might have been worth considering when Gaultois once housed a stinky old fish processing plant of economic importance, but today it makes no sense whatsoever, given that Gaultois is experiencing deathly circumstances similar to what McCallum is.

I learned of this tension between the two towns when I naively questioned why the *Terra Nova* only overnights in Gaultois, and residents of that outport threatened to throw me overboard for asking. It turns out that where a ferry ties up is a matter of convenience, pride, and safety. But don't take my word on it. Ask the gentle giant Donovan Tucker, a skipper from Wareham, Newfoundland, who covers for other skippers around the world when they're sick or in need of a holiday. Donovan says, "As captain, I have to put safety ahead of everything else. So it's my job to consider a worst-case scenario." We are talking in the *Terra Nova's* wheelhouse, a location I feel privileged to be in, given that this area of high responsibility is often off-limits to all but the captain and crew.

"So say you get an emergency call in the night from McCallum and the ferry is tied up in Gaultois," Tucker cautiously articulates. "It would probably take us at least an hour and forty minutes to get her to McCallum. And then we're talking another hour and a half before we get our emergency situation to an ambulance in Hermitage.

"We're also talking about a trip across what is sometimes pretty rough water. There's no guarantee we're going to be able to make that trip without going inside."

"Going inside" refers to a safer, more sheltered, but more time-consuming route around Long Island, but only if winter ice doesn't render that alternative route unnavigable.

Tucker continues, "That means, on a good night, it takes us more than three hours to get an emergency case in McCallum to an ambulance in Hermitage. In comparison, if you have an emergency in Gaultois, you're talking about what could be a twenty-minute ride in a speedboat across what are smoother waters than you'll see on the trip from McCallum.

"Now, I've got nothing against Gaultois. Those people deserve good emergency service too. But it doesn't seem right that the people in one community are looking at a three-hour wait for an ambulance, while the other town is looking at twenty minutes for the same thing. Even if she was tied up in McCallum and we had to go to Gaultois in the night, we're talking about a little more than a two-hour wait for an ambulance for Gaultois people. I'm not saying that's a short time — I wouldn't want to wait two hours — but it is an hour less than what McCallum people face today.

"So, nothing against the people of Gaultois," Donovan patiently repeats, "I'm just thinking about how to reduce the risk of someone getting sick or hurt in McCallum before we could get them medical attention, without costing Gaultois too much of a service they are entitled to too."

Yet Gaultois yaks on. Like when they privately and publicly push for the people of McCallum to lobby for their own ferry, even though such divisive direction doesn't fit with current economic times — an era when provincial governments are insisting municipalities amalgamate.

That's why McCallum residents are recommending that the two towns refine working relationships already in place, insisting the way of the future is about greater cooperation and sharing. The people of McCallum believe that the biggest reason the province is pushing for resettlement is government doesn't want to spend the $50 million required to replace the decrepit *Terra Nova*.

Then there's the confrontational question I most frequently field from Gaultois folks: if the situation was reversed, would you give up and downgrade what little bit of service that you have to help us? To which I can say without hesitation, I most certainly would. It brings me great pleasure to know that, on several occasions in the past, with a couple of ferries out of commission at the same time, the province decided McCallum had to forgo some service in an effort to support people in other isolated communities. Doing so genuinely makes me feel that I am part of the great outport tradition of looking out for the needs of the whole, ahead of the wants of the individual. And if any McCallum residents feel differently about the province's occasional decision to sacrifice service under such circumstances, I don't hear about it. In fact, my family, friends, and I have found that the Newfoundlanders' willingness to share sets them apart from the rest of Canada. But I am no longer blind to the fact that not every rural community thinks the same.

five

The Chair of the McCallum Relocation Committee is in the process of organizing a second expression of interest concerning possible relocation. The Chair said that in a small community like McCallum the required 90 percent vote needed for possible relocation actually means that two or three households can determine whether a community relocates or not. . . . There are eight students in the St. Peters School while there are 27 people in the community in the 25 to 50 range while there are 50 people in the 50 to 80 age group.

— Clayton Hunt, *The Coast of Bays Coaster,*
September 23, 2013

So the natives are restless regarding resettlement. Some are excited at the possibilities, while others are afraid. But both camps contain their share of angry personnel.

Anger has been an influencing factor in my life. My mom and dad were both angry, but it is my father's rage that I remember most. Dad's losses of control were dramatic. Even sober, his fury could fill the house. A shift worker, my father would explode if we woke him up from an afternoon nap. His anger only subsided after he unloaded it on the rest of us. It would take a long time of watching Dad stomp around the house repeating, "Poor Wally Ward," before we finally got some peace. He needed to get over feeling sorry for himself first.

Like many little boys, I copied my father's behaviour. Especially the blaming. I also learned it's okay to inflict your pain on others, and that that act is easier to accomplish if your victim is smaller and weaker than you are. I was unintentionally taught that a male doesn't have to take responsibility for the agony he causes unless he tries his luck on an even meaner man, at which point the instigator should be aware that he is at risk of losing his front teeth.

I remember being eleven years old and crashing and banging around my bedroom, hollering as loud as I could that one day, everybody was going to regret the way they had treated me. Not that anyone ever did anything especially bad — I just felt compelled to tell them that after I ran away, they were all going to wish they could take back every despicable act they'd ever inflicted on me. I pictured hopping a boxcar to British Columbia with a hobo stick over my shoulder — the kind of rucksack I had seen in the comics, with a bandana on the end, tied in such a way that it could carry my belongings. After an extended period of me angrily warning my family about their pending remorse,

I remember Dad saying, "That's enough." He said it in a civil way, but I knew how serious he was. I realized my rant was over. Yet there was never any talk about the source of my anger, the useless way in which I had conducted myself, or how I might approach things differently next time. Nobody on either side of the argument apologized. Maybe Dad thought I was learning manly conduct. Or perhaps he was too insecure to see himself in my destructive behaviour.

No wonder I was so bad at managing my anger throughout my marriage to Janet. I quickly defaulted to feeling sorry for myself, and I never questioned if it was wrong for Janet to fear me. Not that she was ever at any physical risk, but I'm sure she didn't know that.

I loved my anger. It made me feel safe and in control. I remember ripping a door off its hinges. Janet had closed that door in my face. I believe she meant to insult me, but even if she did intend to offend, Janet didn't deserve to be reminded that I was strong enough to destroy that door.

With Carol, I quickly learned that I had to get my anger under control. When you're in a second significant relationship and the same ruinous patterns are repeating themselves, you'd better summon up the courage to look in the mirror. The idea of accusing Carol of being responsible for my anger quickly became unpalatable. So I went to work on studying my psychological shortcomings and gradually learned to recognize my role in our confrontations earlier and earlier.

After seeking considerable professional assistance, and reading several books on the subject, I have learned to identify when anger has a hold on me early enough in the process that I now make smarter choices regarding how I want to respond. Yet I don't believe anger is a bad thing. Quite the opposite, actually — I think anger is good information; it is telling us something is wrong and needs attending to. *My* anger informs me that I'm afraid, that I am in a scary situation I can't control. But how I react to that realization is entirely up to me. How I deal with my rage can be good or bad, so the only action I'll now allow myself is to react responsibly. I no longer want to subject anyone else to my pain.

I know a Newfoundlander who poured hot tea on his wife while she was nursing their daughter. When that girl turned six her father told her, "It's time I taught you your mother is a whore." That guy once steered the family boat between some ridiculously dangerous rocks, with the innocent child in the bow proudly pulling on the painter, while he threatened to sink them all because he'd left his jigger behind and blamed his wife for his forgetfulness. It was only a pretend trip to the store on the part of the mother that got the guiltless out of the house. As it was, it took years of work from that emotionally damaged woman's extended family, a team of pros, a few close friends, and a new partner to keep her from going back to her abuser.

I wonder how that fellow feels about it all now, what with the two most important people in his world living in Gander with another man — a good man — while he sits in a lonely old shed on Trinity Bay. I wonder if the things that guy held onto so tightly — the matters he refused to budge on — seem as important to him as they once did. I too have dug in my heels, and I can't recall what the issues I clung to are anymore. But they sure seemed important to me at the time — so much so that the thought of giving them up made me seethe with senseless anger.

Which brings me back to the amount of anger happening in McCallum around resettlement money. Many who want to accept the government's offer are blaming those who wish to stay for standing in their way. This resentful crowd talks like it's *their* money already, when it is actually only an enticing offer. And those who don't want to go are so mad about the criticism they're receiving for resisting that even if they do see good reason to change their mind, they won't, because of the large anger they hang onto for their accusers. Of course, there is still a crowd that is being classy about it all. McCallum really does contain some elegant individuals.

There are women with domestic talents that border on genius. And the men are amazing at matters like boat repair, fishing, working in the woods, providing for their family, and, more than anything, bravely staring down the dangers that come with life on the sea. Where their weaknesses exist are in discussing matters of emotional importance and voicing opinions — privately facing off or publicly debating bureaucrats, biologists, and businesspeople who use words and legislation more than the mechanical and physical tools these fishing families are familiar with.

I see how this happened. For hundreds of years, outport people have been shamed by those looking for an edge. Politicians, businessmen, mainlanders . . . they've all worked in one way or another to keep rural Newfoundlanders under thumb. They use the age-old trick of making others feel inferior when their language is different or they haven't got a formal education. Townies have bullied baymen for centuries.

One of the biggest contributors towards reducing *my* anger has been the death of my mom and dad. I was in Newfoundland when each took terminally ill. With Dad, who died first, I spoke with him on the phone while he lay in the hospital, but I only returned to Ontario for his funeral, to connect with my siblings. In Mom's case I came home before she passed on, to assist with her care. After both those burials, McCallum's residents greeted my return to Newfoundland with the same two words, "Welcome home." A generous gift that, to this day, consistently causes me to cry.

Caring for Mom was an ordeal. She checked herself out of palliative care, losing her placement in the process, so she could attempt to attend *one* party, making my anger management intentions an enormous challenge to achieve. I realize I should be compassionate (Mom fell trying to take part in that party), but I've always struggled with adults who make choices with no consideration for how they affect others. Especially their children. In my childhood home, it always seemed to me that, as the Ward kids came of age, we made safer day-to-day decisions than our mom and dad did.

Sooner or later, however, we're all forced to learn how tough it is to lose someone of such significance. Right until the end, I only wanted my parents to be pleased with me.

Mom didn't want a send-off. She wanted her body left to science, and she believed that if people wish to honour the dead, they don't need a formal service to do so. Mom also felt that if she couldn't be at the middle of a party, it didn't matter to her whether such an event occurred or not. Yet it took until her final thirty-six hours on earth before she would provide me with that information. Mom wouldn't discuss any aspect of her death. "Believe me," she insisted, "when my time comes, I will go gracefully, but I'm nowhere near needing to discuss death yet." She said this two days before she died.

At the time of my mother's demise, I made sure that those who mattered most to Mom knew of her passing as soon as possible. A month after that, I followed up with a short announcement in her hometown newspaper. That's when people got grouchy, expressing grave concern that Mom wasn't given a proper goodbye. As much as they insisted otherwise, this grumpy group was suggesting that I hadn't honoured my mother's final wishes.

In defense of those who found it impossible to mind their own business, they too were hurting, filled with guilt because they didn't have the courage to visit Mom in the hospital and scared to death regarding the lack of control they have over their own eventual loss of life. As for the timing and content of mom's obit, my heart has no clock. I wasn't going to be forced into following industry-imposed timelines, and I was not ready to comment publicly on my mother's passing. Until now.

June Irene Ward was the oldest of seven Toronto children. Left at eleven years of age in 1942 to raise her six siblings after their mother died at twenty-nine from complications associated with giving birth to her second set of twins, June did a remarkable job of overcoming circumstances that could easily have crushed her. Maybe she acquired such strength from her grandfather who died at Vimy Ridge.

After marrying Wally and then losing her firstborn at birth, June raised a family of five children in Kitchener, Ontario. However, tragedy struck again when the Wards' oldest daughter and her husband, both twenty-six, were killed in a car crash. In response to such heartbreak, Wally went on an angry ten-year binge, and June entered a decade of depression. "Those were dark days," she'd said.

Yet, through it all, June carried on. Her tolerance for pain was extraordinary, and her capacity to put one foot in front of the other in her efforts to connect with her closest friends was a characteristic she demonstrated right up until her death at eighty-three. Predeceased by four siblings, June's cause of death came from a long list of ailments including diabetes, blood clots, heart disease, and cervical cancer. June's earthly belongings were donated to the Salvation Army, an agency that surely aided June and her siblings when *their* mother prematurely passed away.

When my mother's mom died, the idea of anger management was thirty years away. I'm sure those kids were left to fend for themselves and that their colossal losses shaped them. Same goes for my father — an only child — who was born to parents who resented his presence. I can't comprehend how any of them coped.

Even at my dad's death, his anger ruled parts of our lives. The clearest indication of this occurred when everyone realized he had cut me from his will because twenty-four years earlier I'd told him that his drunken behaviour was hurting my mom and little brother. Don't get me wrong, what my father did with his money was his business. But twenty-four years? The last twenty of which he stayed sober, after finally moving out of the family home following a second session in rehab. Some would think twenty clear-minded years was enough time for my father to rethink his hard-headedness, but given the losses and abuses my mom and dad experienced, perhaps I should be surprised that they fared as well as they did. I feel the same way about rural Newfoundlanders — life hasn't been easy for any of them.

six

To the Dunderdale government:

You had to have known what would happen. The Province of Newfoundland has resettled hundreds of communities, so you can't be surprised that by increasing relocation money and insisting that folks within the communities come to a 90% agreement before accessing your offer, that you would be pitting neighbour against neighbour — even family against family.

So now what? What's Plan B now that we've determined that three out of four residents within our community wish to take advantage of your offer but that this is not acceptable for you? What now, now that we've concluded that you want the members of this community to continue to try to influence each other — to do your dirty work — regarding relocation?

In the meantime, our children study and play alone, our doctor visits less often, our population ages, our weather worsens, our capacity to meet the community's physical demands gets harder, our fish prices lower, our fishery and infrastructure weakens, our employment opportunities less sustainable, our access to employment insurance more restrictive, our ferry older, slower, and less frequent, our drinking, bathing, and washing water less acceptable, our friends fewer, our relationships more strained, and our residents more depressed.

So we're asking: how do you plan to support this community now that you've sped up the unraveling process? Please advise us of your plans as soon as possible, because things are falling apart around here.

McCallum's Relocation Committee

— Letter to the editor, *The Harbour Breton Coaster*, October 30, 2013

Everything isn't all well in my world, either. Not that the challenges I'm experiencing are the same as those my McCallum friends are facing, but that I too am affected by my current circumstances; I'm lonely for a significant other. That's why I'm ending this evening like I have so many of late — exploring intimacy online.

I wish you could see her photo. It shows she's fit, and it promotes her beautiful smile. So I'll admit to being male — while perusing online dating profiles, my initial instinct is to assess the photo. But, *un*-guy-like, I've been told, I do read entire profiles. Still, if there isn't a photograph, I don't even begin to investigate.

Outside of the obvious biological forces that make me want to see an image, I get a lot of info from photos.

Bookworm or fitness fanatic? Flower child or business-woman? Not right or wrong, better or worse, or even information I can count on — just a tiny but important piece of the puzzle. Choosing *not* to provide a picture conveys considerable info as well. Communicating with a faceless soul makes me feel unsafe, and I find it bizarre that I have to point this out to women.

Bride understands all this. Bride wastes no time in trusting me. Not unsafely so. She just decides my words are authentic and that, until I prove otherwise, she is going to give me the benefit of the doubt. In the meantime, we are simply trading email messages, and both of us agree that there is nothing about this exchange that needs to be seen as threatening.

As difficult as online dating is, I don't find the email piece overwhelming. I obviously have some writing skills. Plus, present practice suggests that men are expected to spend much time in the early stages of online dating proving that they are what they say they are — a part of the process I accept, given the high number of cowardly males who hide in their parents' or partner's basement pretending to be something that they're not.

Bride shows tremendous confidence and courage. A St. John's mother of three, she wastes no time informing me of her parenting priorities. Yet right behind that announcement, she makes it clear that she would enjoy finding time for me when her kids are with their father, should our introductory discussions present that possibility. Then she quickly goes to work making me feel deserving of a woman's attention, pointing out my strengths and gently supporting me through my weaknesses — a pattern I try to replicate in return.

Rather than show and tell, Bride and I exchange stories that indirectly illustrate who and what we are and photos that present us at our best and worst. We interact — via many messages, and later on the phone — in a fashion that focuses on clear communication. Yet dialogue never leaves anyone wondering whether the connection is anything other than intimate. Not phone sex, thankfully, but adult discussion around subjects like truth and integrity, emotional and physical security, and our personal definitions of intimacy — topics I find fascinating, and guaranteed to turn me on, but not standard practice as it applies to the early stages of online dating as I've experienced it.

I see it in online profiles, how people find the process so scary that they can only manage to write about who they are and what they're after for a few frightful minutes. Imagine a short sloppy sales pitch that focuses on others' shortcomings, because that's what a lot of dating profiles look like — people indirectly complaining about previous partners. It's difficult to believe that some individuals see the creating of an online dating profile as potentially the most important thing they'll ever do. Witnessing this under-estimation of the impact that a shoddy self-portrait can have on your long-term life makes me wonder what baffling behaviours *I've* learned from my culture, parents, and peers that *I'm* unwittingly committing.

Current common belief is that online dating is most effective when the dater works with two sites — one well known and the other some sort of specialty market, maybe a certain philosophy or ethnic or religious group. I find, in Newfoundland, that it works best to choose one site where people have to pay to post their profile and another where such service is free. The paid site because it attracts the kind of people who take the pursuit of a partner seriously enough that they are willing to sacrifice a small fee to achieve their goal, and the free site because that's what 99 percent of Newfoundlander daters prefer.

I often opt to hide my profile, making it available only to those who *I* contact, because generally, what I'm after is not in Newfoundland. Especially when working with data-banks made up of less than a dozen daters. Size matters. Not that what I want is entirely absent. Just that what I require — a woman with an ample imagination who understands why I'm here — is not in Newfoundland in any kind of quantity. So it takes considerable cross-Canada searching for me to find someone who might wish to connect with me. And those women on the mainland who might find me a good fit are not searching Newfoundland profiles. So I file my account in an area that can only be accessed by people I initiate contact with and then I take responsibility for reaching out.

Only occasionally will I put my profile out to the general public. I'll test the waters. Especially if my confidence is low, if I'm having no luck connecting with those who *I* find intriguing. That's when Bride found me — when I briefly went public at a paid online location.

She calls me her delicious secret. She doesn't tell a soul. Nor do I. Not that there are ever any secrets in an outport. Just that, if I want to, I can keep people from knowing where I'm going when I leave. I just lie to them. Telling untruths is only one painful practice you have to work with when your neighbours want to know what you're up to and you don't wish to share.

Getting out of an isolated outport is difficult in other ways as well. Weather must be watched until the day you depart. You never know until the boat shows up if your journey is going to happen, and such unknowns can result in considerable anxiety for even the most seasoned seaman. Some days you can't be sure which form of transportation you'll take — ferry or helicopter — with your choice affecting the amount of baggage you're allowed to bring along.

This trip I travel by helicopter because our ferry has been asked to assist elsewhere — an occurrence I'm grateful for. To look directly down at an incredibly dramatic landscape from twelve hundred feet is an extraordinary experience. It's only from the air that I can see what a large amount of freshwater there is in Newfoundland — at every elevation — because this island's granite underlay refuses to allow rain and runoff to percolate through soil the way less rocky environments do.

Our copter puts down in the Hermitage Lions Club parking lot. I'm ready to roll. I am not immune to cabin fever, and even though my date is days away, I'm overflowing with anticipation. After sharing a few words with the family that permits me to park my car on their property at that end of the ferry line, I hit the road. Not the best of roads, mind you — not as nice as our federal member of parliament's road — but the only route we have.

Three hours' drive to the Trans-Canada Highway and

another five from my ultimate destination, I try to make these trips a good time. Today I travel farther north than normal, to Lumsden, to explore a Newfoundland rarity — a sandy beach. But that outing isn't as much fun as I'd hoped for. Lumsden's beach is littered with noisy toys in various states of disrepair and demolition. Dirt bikes, ATVs, and side-by-sides. Seeing so many motorized vehicles and the children who abuse them reminds me how some parents believe it's okay to simply throw your kids the keys and kick them out the door.

Disappointed that Newfoundland beach life isn't better, I head for the Burin Peninsula, hoping to hop a boat ride to South East Bight, another isolated outport. This outing astounds me when I discover that one third of the population — thirty-four people — in South East Bight have the same last name as I do. We even look similar. It's fun to imagine our English ancestors leaving the same location, with this hardy South East Bight bunch settling on Placentia Bay, while my forefathers and mothers sailed up the St. Lawrence Seaway, just because my gang might have had a couple more quid. It's also a treat to take this trip aboard McCallum's regular runner, the *Terra Nova*, because South East Bight is where she and my friends who work on her have been loaned to while the South East Bight boat is in for refit.

Next stop is Cape St. Mary's Bird Sanctuary, where I see thousands of breeding black-legged kittiwake, northern gannet, common and thick-billed murre, razorbill, black guillemot, double-crested and great cormorant, and northern fulmar. Then I move on to the island's east coast for an anticipated sighting of a rare bird of a different breed — a wide-smiled, slim-bodied beauty.

What do you need to know, dear reader? That Bride is another knockout? Ontario-born and raised to Newfoundland parents, she returned to "The Rock" as a teen, quickly establishing herself as an academic, extracurricular, and work-related success. Cheerful, motivated, and emotionally healthy, Bride welcomes me into her handsome St. John's home like a friend from afar, and a long-lost lover.

The food that fills her fridge is reminiscent of the culture I come from, making the culinary experience she treats me to an infrequent delight. The talented and thoughtful way in which she prepares and presents it all makes me feel special for three highly memorable days.

In noting her attention to detail and eavesdropping on the occasional call from her kids, it's easy to see Bride is an amazing mom. Yet, once she realizes all is well in their world, she quickly returns to showering attention on the two of us. Except for one quick walk around Mundy Pond, we don't go outside the entire time. We simply experience three days of adult indulgence. Yet I don't leave wanting more. I don't mean that my visit wasn't pleasurable (it was) or that parting was easy (it wasn't). We talked extensively about my exit, none of which came without pain. It's just that — and this is where it gets dangerous, speaking for someone else — I believe *we* decided we didn't want a long-term relationship. Yet I should stop talking for another and focus on my own feelings. I can say whatever I want about how I wish to share this journey, but when someone really special ends up in my arms, I don't always entirely engage. This is not the first time that I've experienced this pattern, and I can't keep blaming it on the other — Bride was beautiful, warm, and welcoming.

Maybe I'm struggling to commit, but why would that be? I am truly convinced that almost any couple can succeed if they're willing to do whatever work it takes. So why should I turn and run when I meet up with a winner? Perhaps, after two twelve-year relationships, I now know too much about the energy required to make one work and no longer want to do that drudgery. Yet I believe goodness is the greatest force in the world, and I see it everywhere in my isolated outport and am wanting to once again share in my blessings. So why the struggle? I think it's because physical intimacy with a casual acquaintance is hard on me. It may not be manly to say so, but it's accurate. I'm not relaxed sharing a bed with a near-stranger — even a wonderful one. I believe that *everything* is better with a familiar partner, and that that elation increases over time.

But "time" could be difficult to create from an isolated outport, because I am also having trouble imagining how a relationship will work — St. John's is a ninety-minute boat ride and an eight-hour drive from McCallum, and that's appearing impossible right now. Especially during lobster season. I'm a hypocrite for having suggested otherwise during my online discussions with daters. I'm feeling like a phoney, and I am experiencing enormous anxiety as a result of being so wrong. While I long to once again be intensively involved with a woman, I don't wish to do so at the expense of my McCallum adventure or any part of it. I must get clear about what I want my Newfoundland life to look like, and what kind of price I'm willing to pay for such a journey. In the meantime, I'm telling everyone in McCallum that my helicopter ride was the highlight of my trip, but that too isn't true.

Part Two

seven

I want nothing more than to make the most of my experiences and opportunities. That's why I'm here, in McCallum. I really do want to live life to its fullest and support others who wish to do the same. But most days I'm scared and lonely and unsure how to proceed. And I want to stop pretending otherwise. So it's time I revisited some lessons I learned a long time ago, on another island — on the other side of the world.

I turned twenty-two in Australia. Getting to Oz was not easy. Travelling to Australia was harder than moving to Newfoundland. Some might think that statement obvious, but I don't mean the purchase of an expensive plane ticket, twenty-four-hour travel of ten thousand miles, or my commitment to twelve months down under. It was the quitting of a good Canadian manufacturing job that I found most challenging. I'd been hired full-time at Labatt, bought a house, a truck . . . and everyone was saying, "You can't quit that job."

Brewery work was seen as good employment among the working-class crowd I'd been born into. Wages and benefits were considered exceptional, conditions above average, and in 1980, Labatt had a reputation for treating people right. Plus, my dad had been in the brewery business for decades, so there was another kind of pressure that came along with leaving. Not only was I shunning my father's choices, I was redirecting the family dream — a path that had already experienced massive upheaval when my sister and her husband died the previous year. I've suffered a couple of personal blows and quit several good jobs since, but at twenty-one, that experiential pathway I chose was scary territory.

Escaping to Australia ultimately made my predicament more palatable. The flora and fauna, slower paced way of life, beaches, and, yes, "sheilas," made it much easier to forget what some were saying about my choices. The non-threatening koalas, charismatic cockatoos, and hardy gum trees intrigued me, and the Aussies' attitudes taught me much. Australians distrust established authority but believe in lengthy leaves of absence and the idea that everyone is entitled to "a fair go."

The first thing I did in Australia was connect with an old friend from home. Such familiarity made my gigantic adjustment easier, as did the support group my buddy had acquired upon *his* arrival. My friend was playing hockey in Melbourne, where his team found me accommodation and a factory job. As usual, life would have been much more challenging if not for the kindness of others. Then my matey and I went to work reinforcing a friendship that has lasted a lifetime. We suntanned, snorkelled, boated, worked hard, walked the beach, body-surfed, made money to survive, threw a Frisbee for endless hours, missed our families and friends, drove on the wrong side of the road, attended concerts and sporting events, learned new words, ate foreign foods, sheared sheep, shared John Lennon's death, camped extraordinary country, travelled further . . . for an entire year. Thus, the most lasting lesson of my Australian journey has been the part where I learned that calculated risk can reap great rewards, yet I still need to force myself to live that scary lesson every day.

So it is time I upped the ante, further embracing everything about this Newfoundland leg of my journey. Not that facing fear is for everyone, or that others should confront their feelings as frequently as I do. Just that, however you define safety, stepping outside your comfort zone can facilitate enormous growth and inspire considerable creativity. Looking back, quitting so-called secure work and travelling to Australia at twenty-one taught me the most indelible lessons I ever learned. Lessons without which I would never have made it to McCallum. I wouldn't have become a writer either. In the early stages of my writing life, I felt a large lack of confidence. To this day, I don't know an adverb from an adjective, and I often use a rural vernacular that many insist is improper and poorly suited for nonfiction. I hate being told that my emotional style makes my audience uncomfortable, and it angers me every time someone suggests I edit my anger.

Writing my first book was an act of daily desperation for me. I had to trust my previous experiences long enough to get words onto the page, but given writing is such an isolated undertaking, I found this deed difficult and lonely. Every day, I self-sabotaged in one way or another. Still do.

With an uncommon idea, a style unlike others', a fear of failing, and an inadequate understanding of what needs to happen next, my creative efforts require as much reading as writing while I move through unfamiliar territory. But even books from the masters aren't enough — I occasionally need to look a published author in the eye and experience others who are struggling to achieve the same goals that I am.

An education hack, I frequently take courses. Then an award-winning author tells me writing workshops are a waste of time — writers just need to write. While I understand why some say this — that time devoted to telling others that you want to write might be better spent writing, rather than trying to fight your fears by commiserating with your peers — I think the idea of connecting with people who look at writing dilemmas differently than I do is more promising than naysayers know. So I sought out the teachers at Piper's Frith, a secluded writers' workshop found at the top of Newfoundland's Burin Peninsula, just west of Come By Chance and south of Goobies.

As good as Piper's leadership was, I had more in common with my classmates — everyday people feeling doubts about their dreams. My fellow students didn't disappoint. The appetite I witnessed for genres I'd previously ridiculed was a humbling experience. Science fiction, poetry, humour, even horror. My classmates were crazy about their respective areas of expertise, and their support of my obscure interests was endearing. We laughed, critiqued, cringed — even cried — in response to each other's priceless opinions.

My mentor — Newfoundland novelist Kevin Major — was terrific, my roommate a gentleman, and my support group second to none. The location was incredible, and we ate like royalty. The Newfoundland network I was introduced to, and have accessed since, was worth every penny of Piper's price. I learned more about the publishing industry over coffee and cake than I ever could have on my own. I went back to McCallum believing I was a way better writer.

So think what you want about synchronicity — my life today wouldn't look at all like it does if I hadn't gone to Australia when I did. I would not have had the confidence to build on the successes I've achieved since. And I wouldn't have seen the sights I have, sights like the Sydney Opera House, the Great Barrier Reef, and the all-powerful Pissing Horse.

The Pissing Horse is an enormous waterfall on Newfoundland's southwest coast. A couple of kilometres west of the ghost town Richard's Harbour, Pissing Horse is seldom seen. It's experienced by less than a dozen people per year, and the only reason I get to see this magnificent natural beauty as often as I do is because I work on a boat that puts lobster pots around its base for five weeks every spring.

Named for the way in which a steady, full-bodied stream explodes from its head, anyone who has seen a stallion discharge will understand the similarity. Except you can't see Pissing Horse's source — it's almost a thousand feet high. I picture it approaching liftoff, with considerable power, along a restricted channel at a slightly upward angle. I imagine there is a strong, secure rock in place at the point of climax for the leading edge of that cliff to have remained so rigid under load for so long.

Contemplating Pissing Horse's scale, however, is a difficult concept to consider. When the only man-made objects for miles around are you and your little boat, it is nearly impossible to grasp just how large the landscape is. There are days when this gigantic geology, made up of magnificent multi-coloured mountains and cliffs stripped of soil by a relentless flow of ice almost fifty thousand years ago, swallows me up. Measuring and banding lobsters, filling bait bags, tuning out the skipper's abusive barking, and trying to stay standing when too much sea tries to beat us against the shore occasionally consumes me. Yet, in the brief moments when I return to the present and look at Pissing Horse after what seems like a long time, I see we have barely moved from where I thought we were thirty minutes earlier. It seems like, in reality, we have a high-powered outboard motor steadily moving us east, but in the magically huge world where I work, it looks like we've gotten nowhere.

Facheux Bay is another beauty that I feel blessed to know. An ancient fiord that sits four kilometres west of McCallum and runs ten kilometres inland, Facheux is the jewel in the crown called the Southwest Coast. The best way to describe Facheux is to say that it looks like Gros Morne National Park — an area that has caught the world's attention because of all its natural beauty. Gros Morne is the landmark that the province of Newfoundland, via television, newspapers, magazines, and the internet, endlessly invites the world to visit. Yet there are a lot of landscapes on the Southwest Coast that are akin to Gros Morne. Locations like Goblin Head, Hare Bay, the Devil's Dancing Table . . .

Facheux Bay is the most dramatic example of what the Southwest Coast has to offer when it comes to heart-stopping topography. Yet, Facheux has a fascinating human history as well. Not only did Captain James Cook tie up in Facheux Bay, many Newfoundland and native cultures used this glaciated inlet for winter sustenance.

One hundred-year-old tale occasionally told is about the trapper Henry Buffett, who died in his sleep on Facheux's historic hills. When Henry didn't wake, his dog, perhaps in an effort to stir his master — lick, lick, nudge, nudge, and eventually a playful bite or two — damaged Henry's head. Or maybe the dog, after a lengthy period of loyally lying alongside its master's remains, acted on its natural instincts instead of starving to death.

Whatever the dog's intentions, a group of men later found Henry's faithful four-legged friend and followed it back to Buffett's body. Assuming the dog could not be trusted after acquiring the taste of human flesh, the men shot it before burying Buffett. Today, many believe it was unnecessary to dispose of the dog, but a century ago, we viewed such situations differently.

Another story that illustrates how insanely we've seen the world tells how a McCallum foursome sailed up Facheux in a dory, stumbled across an indigenous woman working alone, and promptly drowned her in a saltwater pond. Not all the detail regarding this tragic story is clear, but no one denies that native life was once horrifyingly and senselessly seen as dispensable.

Trips from McCallum to Facheux Bay today begin with fighting through the choppy seas and various tides that collect around Taylor Island. As scary as this experience can be for me, I always take a few seconds to consider how challenging life must have been for the three families that lived on Taylor Island in the late 1800s. I pay a quiet tribute to the fact that our entire crew, including me, is here because of one of those families. Carol's grandmother Cora and her twin brother, Sandy — the late patriarch of McCallum's Feaver family — were born on Taylor Island in a small bay called Indian Cove. The Feavers are my go-to crew for adventure.

With the sun still a long way from coming up over Canada, I start clapping my heavily gloved hands in an effort to bring life to my already chilled-to-the-bone body. Once the rugged beauty of Back Cove is behind us, I try to spot a big seal on Little Shag Rock. I love witnessing wild-life. But fishermen curse seals for their capacity to consume fish. Fishers also resent the fact that much of the world despises Newfoundland for slaughtering baby seals for their fur. Many men take this rejection personally, to the point where they try to kill the animals whenever they can. So seal sightings also sadden me, because every minute that fish-ermen are upset with a seal is sixty seconds when they're not angry at a government incapable of caring for a fishery that once provided for all. As for any inconsequential seal killings committed for rage-related reasons, angrily aiming a firearm at *anything* is an insane thing to do.

But a trip up Facheux demands mindfulness, so I redirect my melancholy to the high country and try to imagine giant glaciers scattering multi-storey rocks on smooth summits. I concentrate on the climbing escarpment and, because I get great pleasure from watching pelagic birds, I count the number that call these cliffs home — colourful puffins, gorgeous gannets, elusive turrs, copulating cormorants . . . Then I take my turn on lookout, which, because it's so critical to the well-being of all onboard, is a crazy place to put a come-from-away who can't tell a sunker from a jumper. In search of sentinel assistance, I conjure up the ghost of Captain Cook, who, on June 7, 1766, after anchoring for six days in what today is called McCallum, directed his men to take the same route we are. I wonder how many magnificent mornings the crew of the *Grenville* witnessed and how my skipper today will find his way to the bottom of Facheux Bay through what is still largely darkness and danger. Then an awe-inspiring lip of light forms over Dragon Bay when a full moon falls into an opening between cloud cover and mountaintop, shining a gleaming stream on the water's surface in such a way that all we have to do is find the faith to trust it.

eight

"Your address?" she asks. We're talking on the telephone.

"Post Office Box 3, McCallum, Newfoundland, A0H 2J0," I reply. "Would you like me to spell McCallum for you?"

"I need your street address, sir."

"I'm sorry, I don't have one."

"I need the street name and number on the building you want us to send your parcel to," she repeats in that odd way that is neither offensive nor friendly. It's just — *there*. The kind of voice that sounds more like an automated answering machine than it does a breathing human being.

"Yes, I understand what you're asking for," I say. "It's just that I live in an isolated Newfoundland outport, where there are no streets, resulting in no street names or house numbers. I'm a ninety-minute boat ride from the nearest road."

"I need a street address or the courier won't be able to find your home," she insists.

I stifle a laugh. Sort of. "No courier will be coming here, my dear. I can guarantee you that. Plus, my neighbours and I have ordered many couriered packages previously, using nothing more than the PO Boxes that Canada Post provides, and the items we order always arrive."

"Sir, our system only allows us to enter a street name and house number."

"Okay, that's another story — that's more about insufficient software than it is your resistance to new knowledge, so I'll give you a fake address. It will implicate us both in federal mail fraud, but I'll gladly lie to you if that's your employer's preference."

Silence.

My move. "Oh, look at that! I've got an address right here: 23 Jas Rose Point [or 16 Long Shore Road, or . . .], McCallum, Newfoundland A0H 2J0."

"Spell McCallum please."

Fact is, you can send mail to "The Feller from Away, A0H 2J0," and it will reach me. There are seventy-nine people at this postal code. None live more than a kilometre from everyone else. I'm sure our postmistress, Sharon Feaver, can figure it out.

Despite government efforts to kill us off, Canada is a big country that still contains a considerable rural population. It's easy to forget this when you live in a large urban centre, where services are readily available and geared to meet the needs of the majority.

Try taking out home insurance when you live where I do, when the service provider needs to know if your foundation is full-height poured cement or a cinderblock crawl space. My house doesn't have a foundation, I say. It sits on sticks. What I don't tell them is, when my washing machine is on spin, a few of those pillars shake like loose shingles in an Ontario tornado. I don't point out, "That's my kettle on the stove that you hear rattling right now."

It's impossible to find a technician who can fix the faulty appliance that you purchased new the previous week. And good luck getting a mortgage when the lender asks how far you are from the nearest fire station. Even the federal gun registry isn't set up to serve you, but I don't recommend you use the word "fraud" with those guys.

None of these inconveniences is the end of the world, of course, but the lack of support regarding essential services can wear a person down after a while. All rural Canadians are marginalized in one way or another. They feel insignificant when the system is unaware of their plight and unworthy when others aren't motivated to think outside the box on the rural resident's behalf.

While far from perfect, I try to be aware of the day-to-day damage that results from *my* resistance to seeing the world in new and equitable ways, and I occasionally make an effort to initiate personal behavioural modifications in response. I say that "I occasionally make an effort" to change because doing so is always ultra-difficult. That's why I don't make New Year's resolutions, because I find them too hard to keep. I think that recognizing the end of one year and the start of another helps me to count my blessings and consider my future, but if I wish to implement meaningful change, I don't see the good in starting such a rigorous journey on a culturally assigned day. I believe that the best time for me to act on my ambitions should be based on *my* needs, not some calendar date that coincidentally arrives on one of the darkest days of the year, after a lengthy period of time when many of us have consumed insane amounts of food and alcohol and thrown away any semblance of healthy sleeping habits. I've learned that by establishing January 1 as the day to begin important projects, I won't be in a good position to face the real possibility of needing to get on and off the wagon several times throughout the process. The date I set to spark change has to help me find all the stick-to-it toughness that I can assemble, if I hope to have any success at all.

I do, however, use the changing of the calendar year to reflect on my Newfoundland lifestyle, like how much I enjoy the many hours I spend alone reading and writing in my little McCallum home. I recall the fear that came with moving here, and I smile at the thought of all the supportive calls and emails I receive from those I care about on the mainland. I remember the McCallum folks who frequently feed me, and I dream of further travelling Newfoundland, continuing to use this community as my basecamp. From Stephenville to St. John's, up and down the Northern Peninsula, all along the northeast shore, and south to St. Pierre, I'd never have seen what I have without the stability that McCallum provides.

More than anything though, I smile at the thought of all the days I spend at sea, because that's a large part of what my

Newfoundland life is. I *love* the open ocean. As physically punishing as ocean excursions are, they bring me extreme joy. A rough and tough boat ride makes me feel very much awake in this world. I'm convinced that my time on the North Atlantic Ocean will be one of the more satisfying things that I think about while lying on my deathbed one day.

But with an awareness that I won't always be able to take the beating that comes with life on the sea comes the conscious knowledge that I'm nowhere near willing to give this adventurous world up. So while I resist New Year's resolutions, I do believe in recurring commitments, including one that I have to consistently maintain and continuously improve upon — the need to take care of myself. It's always been day-to-day for me. I'm an excessively greedy eater. If there is fat, salt, or sugar in my home, I'll inhale it. Yet taking the pounding that comes with life at sea requires a strong back, a healthy heart, loose limbs, and an alert brain. Achieving these qualities requires regular exercise, good food choices, and a curious mind — a way of living worth nurturing because I dream of participating in bodily challenging adventures for as long as life will let me.

In fog thick as motor oil, no one knows where we are. I ask the man who does the driving why we aren't carrying a compass. "The man who does the driving" is Junior Feaver, husband of Sharon, McCallum's previously noted postmistress. Junior and Sharon are not thrilled at the thought of seeing their name in print, so I do what I can to respect their concerns, without it costing me my story. This modesty that the two of them demonstrate is not uncommon in McCallum. Lloyd and Linda Durnford share a similar refrain, as does Sarah Fudge's husband, Matt. So, know that despite my occasional underuse of certain individuals' names, these people are incredibly important players in my narrative.

"The swell is always from the sou'west, so I know where we are," Junior patiently points out. "I just don't know *where* we are." I take this to mean he could easily find land if he had to, but he can't guarantee where along that coastline we currently are. So, as we move through fog towards unidentified terra firma, no one knows what dangers sit below the surface. Given the seriousness of the situation, I decide not to ask how anyone can possibly read what direction the swell is coming from this morn, because with the sea so incredibly calm, the roll of the ocean is unreadable.

Junior cuts the engine and signals for quiet. He wants to see if he can hear water flowing against or over any rocks that might be too close for comfort. He can. But that critical realization is temporarily shelved when he spots me peering into the fog beyond the port side. "See something, Dave?" he asks.

"I thought I did," I reply. "But perhaps I am wrong . . ."

Then it resurfaces — a forty-ton humpback whale, its hump a whole lot higher than me. Its massive tail, as it gives us a great wave, is a stunning mosaic of whites and greys. I dream of such sightings, and I'm excited that I'm the guy who spotted it first, because both events are rare; I simply don't understand aquatic ecology like the rest of this gang does. They know so much more than me about where to look for action.

"Whoo-hoo!" I scream, and throw my arms in the air. But my quick-thinking, fast-acting, early forties skipper isn't so thrilled. These fifty-foot marine mammals and the way they so suddenly fill the surface of the sea can easily flip a twenty-two-foot fibreglass boat and everybody in it. "You won't be whoo-hooing if we hit her," Junior firmly informs me as he efficiently works to move our vulnerable vessel out of harm's way. "No sir, you won't be so happy if we hit her."

Then *another* appears. Another humpback. This one astern of the starboard. It is Junior who first sees the second one. Slightly smaller, but right alongside our boat, the possibility of disaster is no less unsettling. We're surrounded. If I didn't have great confidence in my captain, I'd have good reason to worry. Instead I am having fun watching sea monsters in the Gulf of St. Lawrence.

Opening day was another eye-opener. It felt like I was staring down the devil. The roar of the sea was thunderous, and the suck of the landwash awful. It was the worst weather I'd ever been in. As one veteran seaman from another crew kindly told me at the time, "You probably won't see worse unless you get caught in something, because we don't go out in worse than that." In fact, if it hadn't been opening day, I don't believe we would have gone at all. We had a lot of pots to put in, and catching lobsters is competitive. So much so that if we fall behind, we'll even work the occasional Sunday, an otherwise blasphemous act.

People from away don't realize how small our boats are. They think we steam around in large longliners instead of little open motorboats. When it's really rough, we travel in pairs — two boats keeping an eye on each other, just in case. That's when I see what we're up against, when I look over at our neighbour's boat beside us and note that the only components touching the sea are their two heavy outboards and a couple feet of fibreglass while the rest of their vessel hangs ten off a fifteen-foot wave. So it's easy to imagine that *our* boat is doing the same.

The wave action throws me around like I'm a tiny bag of lobster bait. But I'm not scared. Not that I'm not careful or aware of what could happen. Just that I think there is something that occurs in a physical crisis where my mind recognizes that panic is not going to be of any assistance and tells my body to get down to business. It's only when I reflect a week or two later that I allow myself to realize what a wild time I've just lived through.

It *is* quite an operation — a father, four sons, and a mainlander, while Mom makes sure there is pea soup waiting when we get home. Or, as the old folks say about eating pea soup on Saturdays, we celebrate the devil's birthday — a tenet I don't trust, because I saw the devil that day, and he had no interest in partying. All he wanted to do was stir up trouble on thunderous seas and introduce me to a new level of danger.

There was a time in my Ontario life when I climbed trees for a living, carrying a running chainsaw with me as I went. I've assisted with the recovery of avalanche victims in Alberta and lowered skiers from dangling wires and tall towers when their gondola blew off in big winds. I worked at Ground Zero, New York, after the World Trade Center fell and everyone was still sensitive to the potential of another terrorist attack. Still, I believe commercial fishing is the most dangerous job in the world.

Police and firefighters have their moments where they see some horrible things, and, according to injury compensation claims, stevedores and demolition workers are frequently hurt at work. But braving the open ocean is clearly the riskiest job I've ever come across. For men and women to take on tasks that don't pay enough to buy the best boats, technology, or safety wear is ambitious and brave. To go out in unpredictable weather over water so cold that, even if the fishers *could* swim, would kill them quite quickly is courageous.

I tell Junior, when he crawls out over our outboard motor to remove an errant rope from the propeller, "If you slip overboard, don't worry, because I'll have a gaff stuck in you before you know you're wet. I'll jam that sharp hook in your neck, kidney, or crotch," I insist, "and I'll pull you back on this boat before anyone notices you're gone. So don't you be afraid, old buddy — you've got the feller from away watching out for you."

nine

Jupiter's gone missing. Not the planet — the dog. Jupiter is an orange and white Brittany. Some say Brittany spaniel, but the breed has more in common with a pointer than a spaniel, so people who know more about dogs than I do refer to Jupiter as a Brittany.

We're walking Facheux Bay's eastern ridge, a gorgeous stretch of coastal hills, ranging from 700 to 950 feet above sea level. We're partridge hunting. Ptarmigan, actually. Me,

Jupiter, and Jupiter's master, Junior. This is a new experience for me. Hunting, I mean.

As long a distance as we've walked, Jupiter has instinctively run ten thousand times farther, simply doing what bird dogs do — searching for birds. Only a fool would be angry at him for getting lost, assuming that's what's happened. But Jupiter isn't lost. He has two birds in his range and is staring them down, and probably has been for fifteen minutes. It feels like it has taken forever to find him, but Junior has spotted Jupiter on the horizon, among thousands of tiny patches of snow and thousands of big boulders.

Having walked so far already, neither of us is terribly excited about the distance and the technically difficult terrain that stretches between us and this dog. That's why Junior says with a sigh, "You stay here, old boy, and I'll go see what he's got." But I don't want any part of any plan that leaves me behind. I believe we're all in this together, and I tell Junior this. To which he says, while handing me his half-choked, un-cocked, twelve-gauge shotgun, "Then you go. And I'll stay here. Just don't shoot Sharon's dog, Dave."

How long it takes for me to reach that dog and the two partridges he's pinned, I have no idea. My heart is in my throat, so it seems like seconds to me. And sure enough,

Jupiter is right on top of his prey, leaving me no choice but to stir up those birds and fire on the fly.

One lucky shot, one not-so-lucky bird, one special memory. Thanks to the efforts and patience of one talented dog.

It reminds me of a time when I had a dog of my own — a Landseer Newfoundlander. Rudyard was a sweet, handsome, hundred-and-forty-pound pal who loved his walks and swims as much as any canine could. One winter day, the two of us were strolling along the eastern shore of Central Ontario's Sturgeon Lake when I fell with a thud on some thinly snow-covered ice. Slightly winded, I laid there for a few seconds watching Rudyard unwittingly sniff his way through snowdrifts about 100 feet in front of me. Then I thought, because the Newfoundland breed has a reputation for being a rescue dog, it will be interesting to see how my big buddy responds to any indication that I'm incapable of carrying on. Suddenly Rudyard saw me lying on that ice, ran back as fast as he could, and straightaway started humping me.

East Bay by daylight — that's our goal — and then we'll walk as far as Salmon River, which, I learn upon arrival, is not a river at all. It's a freakish site — a long, wide clearing of weathered rock and nothing more, the river killed off decades ago by the province of Newfoundland when they dammed it for hydro.

I've never seen anyone lust for a love affair with large hydro like a Newfie politician does. Newfoundland leaders can't seem to learn from their own history. Like the way they insist on continuously selling off their natural resources at reduced rates, all the while locking themselves into Hoover Dam–like debt. They seem stunted — like an elected official from another era. Maybe they're insecure. It's not difficult to see how they've been taken advantage of over the years. I'm sure many businessmen from the mainland find the Newfoundlanders' vulnerability comical, and profitable, while the ratepayers of Newfoundland and Labrador lose their shirts and their ancient rivers, and salmon lose their lives — billions of salmon that were genetically programmed to swim to the bottom of East Bay but no longer do, because of dimwitted politicians.

We're searching for moose — another Newfoundland staple — but all we've seen is an enormous black bear, a lot of mergansers, and a dead porpoise that's drifted ashore. I get excited about this skeletal discovery, which annoys

Junior when I audibly express my joy. "We're here to *hunt* moose," he quietly scolds me. "Not scare them away."

I don't know how anybody can call what I'm doing hunting. The entire time I'm on the hills, my eyes are focused on my feet. I can't stop staring at the uneven ground on which I intend to place my next step. One foot in front of the other is all I can concentrate on. The moose I am supposed to be looking for might be right beside me, but I wouldn't notice because all I can see is the next hazardous rock, treacherous tree root, and slippery mud puddle.

Something directly beside me that I *deliberately* don't pay attention to is the steep drop towards the sea. Yet I am the only one overwhelmed by my whereabouts. Clyde Feaver has seen it all before — today is just another wonderful walk in the woods for that delightful man. An enviable blend of ancient adult wisdom and childlike joy, Clyde is like no one I've ever known, in the woods, workshop, kitchen, on the sea — a career fisherman, ask Uncle Clyde what he enjoys doing in his spare time and he instantly answers, "Fish." (In Newfoundland, the term Uncle, when used by a non-relative, is done so with the intent to bestow the highest amount of respect on the designated male.)

Junior and Sharon — Clyde's son and daughter-in-law

— aren't concerned about our daunting environment either. Junior is always up for a hike, and Sharon, with her long blond flow tucked tightly up under a pink Ducks Unlimited cap, is quite content to be cradling her rifle. It makes me laugh, the way people who have never seen Sharon react when I share a photo. "Oh . . . she's g-g-gorgeous," they stammer. Like women who hunt aren't supposed to be beautiful. I wish they could see how badly this mother of one wants to help her extended family get the moose that the licence in her pocket entitles her to. A possibility that lurks every time she's on the hunt, because Sharon's a strong hiker, a tenacious tracker, and an extremely accurate shot.

I'm high on the hill. He's deep in the valley but walking straight at me. I can see him through my spyglasses. His antlers alone probably weigh forty pounds. I can't fathom carrying such a load on my head, or trying to fit that large rack between trees. The flap of skin and tuft of hair that hangs from his throat is also quite pronounced. His muzzle and body are black, but I suspect his coat appears much darker than usual because he's just slipped out of the water, an action he accomplished with ease. That's my biggest surprise — his light-footedness. A male eastern moose can weigh fourteen hundred pounds and stand six feet at the shoulder. This critter is clearly in that category. I didn't expect him to be so agile.

His front legs, longer than his back, render him capable of clearing fallen trees — another feat I watch him painlessly perform. I'm surprised at the distance he covers in such a short time, but I shouldn't be — he is on a hunt of his own. He's looking for a cow, and it's not hard to figure out what he wants to do when he finds one. It's all about his biology, and today it's ruling him. So much so that he won't feed — he'll spend his entire time searching for a sweetie-pie. But bulls don't pair-bond permanently. They stay with the cow only long enough to breed before going in pursuit of another partner.

My teammates estimate this animal is twelve years old. I can see how he might have survived such a long time — he blends in with the fall shadows found in deep gullies and along crooked brooks. Many a hunter could have missed him.

While moose can live to be twenty, it's still remarkable that this one is as old as he is, because there are several ways that a moose can die before he reaches the size of this sucker. Black bears are significant predators of moose calves until the calves are nine weeks old, and there are a lot of black bears in Newfoundland. There are also a lot of foolishly fast drivers who hit huge numbers of moose every year.

Given the province issues thirty thousand moose licences annually, twelve years is a long time for a moose to avoid being cut down — a fate this beast seems destined to meet today, until he suddenly turns back into the brook and heads up the hill away from us. Junior thinks that this handsome male caught whiff that not only are there are no fertile females for him to frequent, but there is an ugly old Ontario guy sitting high on the hill.

Turns out it takes us another four days of hiking some highly challenging hills before Sharon finally bags us a big bull. The Feavers give me a large portion of that catch. I know they see it as payment for my contribution to the hunt, but I don't need the feed. I'm sure I won't go hungry. Lots of people give me plenty, and it's not why I participate. I should simply say "no thank you" and note that I'm just glad for the experience and appreciate being invited along. But I don't refuse my friends' attractive offer — I have plans for that meat.

There is no better moment for me than when I can deliver a section of moose to Lloyd and Linda Durnford, the family that most frequently feeds me. It brings me great pleasure to drop a parcel off at that incredible couple's house. Lloyd's a loving teddy bear of a man who likes to pretend he's tough as leather, while Linda is a thoughtful, caring woman with extraordinary household and office skills despite dealing with rickets her entire life. Linda's stamina is second-to-none. She gets more done in a day than I do a month.

My first moose-hunting experience was with Lloyd, after he shot a five-hundred-pound cow south of Pushthrough and needed a team to help carry out his catch — a posse I was proud to be part of, but, with no previous experience in what was required, I felt lost. I thought long and hard about the slaughter that awaited us and how I'd feel about it. It turned out that while I'd never seen animal innards on such terms before, I found them more fascinating than offensive. Even the way the men hacked out the organs and chopped through the bones with sharp axes, I found more engrossing than gruesome. Or so I said at the time, afraid that if I told anyone otherwise, I'd never fit in in McCallum.

The parts that needed to be removed as soon as possible to keep them from contaminating the corpse were gone. Held together by thirty pounds of thick skin, what was left had started to stiffen, making Lloyd's moose increasingly unbendable. Movement seemed impossible to me. So I stayed out of the way while my mates carved that body into a condition suitable for transportation. Then the fun began — the actual carrying of the carcass. I found the up and down of it all difficult and the on-and-off-the-boat part nearly impossible. The physical force that was required to carry four enormous portions of dead weight over what the other men insisted was a wimpy distance was a marathon to me. Stumbling around in rubber boots, we climbed across rocks, hills, and brooks, around trees and over cliffs, carrying our load on our backs, on our shoulders, and in our arms.

That style of Sherpa work does not come natural to me. There are parts of the pursuit that I'm just not familiar with — like what to do next, and why. One of the most frustrating parts of this predicament is very few of my neighbours try to teach me. Not that they have bad intentions. It's just that when you live in a community where everyone shares so much common knowledge, it's easy for others to incorrectly assume that you know the same things they do. They always stare at me in authentic amazement when they discover otherwise.

So with every passing season, my backcountry inadequacies slowly melt away, yet I'm still not comfortable with watching a moose die — how long it takes before a bull leaves its feet, even after a large bullet has passed through its lungs. I find it difficult to watch a beautiful creature fight for its life. If we didn't have six Feaver freezers to fill, I would want no part of this killing game. Hunting is not a sport to me — it's all about seeking sustenance in an isolated outport.

Having said that, I have no patience for folks who take an anti-hunting stance while continuing to consume animal products. Don't these eaters of flesh who object to *all* hunting ever wonder where their meat comes from? Do they know how hideous the trip to the slaughterhouse is for the animals they consume? Some travel thousands of miles in the back of a trailer over several days, sloshing around in their own excrement.

Have you ever considered what the kill floor looks like in a meat plant, how your supper's final days and hours are a more terrifying experience than some moose's final minutes in a Newfoundland marsh, where all he is thinking about is sex? Have you ever imagined the factory environment your chicken and cow products come from or the densely populated cages your salmon *sort of* swam in? "I prefer not to think about it," the anti-hunting animal-eating crowd often say when I challenge their consumption patterns. Cowards, I call them.

We should all have to look our meat in the eye at some point on its journey. We should all have to answer to the fact that most of our meat, chicken, and fish live an existence that's entirely about profit for the producer and convenience and cost efficiency for the consumer, at the expense of the animals living a horrific life. In the meantime, I'll sleep better knowing that the meat I'm eating came from a moose that lived free-range on birch and willow shoots and aquatic plants, was shot by a woman who stood three hundred yards away at the time of pulling the trigger, and cleaned by five families that expect to eat every part possible.

ten

I joke that I'm a Sherpa, but that's not an accurate thing to say. Sherpas are renowned for their mountaineering skills. My talents are not mountaineering related. Plus, while Sherpa work is wonderful, I want a bigger part of the hunt, and that's not very Sherpa-like of me.

I phone Ontario's natural resources office in search of proof that I'd previously passed their hunter education course. I took that class at a time when I taught conservation ecology to students who dreamed of obtaining the same qualification. After a couple of wild goose chases — you can always tell when you're talking to a civil servant who doesn't give a damn — I finally find someone who can send a letter indicating I successfully completed that course. This confirmation is useful because obtaining equal education in Newfoundland will prove costly if I need to book accommodation in Corner Brook, where classes are currently offered.

Newfoundland and Labrador's environment and conservation office requested that letter after I asked how someone goes about getting his first moose licence. While acquiring this document guarantees nothing, it thrills me that I'm one step closer to contributing to McCallum in another highly meaningful way.

I buy a blaze-orange cap to help keep me safe and better-fitting boots to assist with my hiking. I also read a story in *Outside* magazine about a new kind of hunter. Because of a lack of faith in a food web designed to be dependent on ever-increasing gas prices, these modern-thinking hunters are part of a healthy crowd who want to eat only local meat. They no longer wish to consume food that scientists have screwed with. Plus, they're athletic — choosing to hunt high country and shunning the idea of shooting from a truck. They also hold high-tech clothing in high regard. Rejecting the idea that cotton is best in the backcountry, they're spending money on underwear engineered to wick water away from your body. This keen group of carnivores has taken gear normally used by mountain climbers and made it their own. Many are even choosing to hunt with a bow, further distancing themselves from the gang packing gunpowder. I don't want to part with my .303 as long as I'm in rural Newfoundland — I've seen how difficult it is to bring a big animal to the ground — but I do respect those looking for more appreciative ways to participate in the hunt.

McCallum people simply see guns as tools. They don't view firearms as being a whole lot different than a reciprocating saw or an axe. I remember the first time I saw a gun sitting outside Fudge's Store. The gun's owner didn't want to carry his rifle into the shop but saw no reason it couldn't lean unloaded against the front facade while he grabbed a few groceries. I'm sure I was the only person who noticed. For the rest of McCallum, it was just another day in an isolated outport, like someone had stood a muddy shovel against the wall. Even store management couldn't have cared less.

Fudge's Store is the town hub, the place where information is posted, everything from boil-water warnings to church schedules. Employing seven, Fudge's plays an important role in moving, and keeping, money in McCallum. So whatever it is you're after — molasses, veggies, ice cream, gift wrap, a last-second supper spice, pharmaceuticals, a half pound of screws, a bottle of bourbon, or a lottery ticket — chances are you'll find it at Fudge's Store. Unless you're looking for fresh fish.

The first time Carol and I arrived in McCallum, we wanted to purchase fresh fish more than anything but couldn't. Imagine a fully functioning fishing village with an outstanding midsize store — and no seafood for sale. Because with everyone so self-sufficient, outport people have no reason to pay for their fish. Even those without a boat have their sources for seafood. But Carol and I had no such network — we were new and unknown, and people were wary of us. Even when we did find someone with fish to share, they generously refused to take our money, unintentionally making us feel like dependents in a community where we were desperate to prove ourselves otherwise.

Our first source of fish was Lloyd Durnford, but Carol and I agreed we couldn't keep asking Lloyd and Linda for free food. So when McCallum's Kevin Wellman — the community's middleman between fishermen and industry buyers — offered to ask the fishers on our behalf if they had a cod or two they might part with, we happily said thank you. Two hours later, Kevin called saying he had what we were looking for, so I ran to the wharf where our catch awaited. After taking some teasing for the way I carried those cod and doing everything I could to make sure no one would witness my unskillful efforts to clean them, I headed up the road, excited about our bounty. But before I left the harbour, I asked Kevin who the donor was — whom we should thank for our lovely meal. "Lloyd Durnford," he said. Carol and I could have cried. Fortunately for us, Lloyd and his family found this funny, and my clumsy efforts to take care of myself have been a source of humour for outport people ever since.

One of the first things that people lose when they change cultures is their humour. Not that their talent for telling a joke disappears, but because no one in their new culture finds them familiar, a large component of a person's funniness vanishes. So the wannabe comic gradually gives up. I experienced this in Australia. I discovered that few Aussies found me funny, but the day I landed back in Ontario, I was considered comical again. Newfoundland was no different. Of course, the longer I am in McCallum, the more we understand each other. But I'll always be unsure about local custom to one degree or another, and whether my one-liners are going to work or not.

The biggest laugh I get in McCallum occurs when I can deliver a comeback in the direction of someone teasing me about the amount of food I consume. It might be at a community gathering — Canada Day, for example, or a fiftieth wedding anniversary — but when I return to my table with an extra helping of pasta loaded with lobster, someone is guaranteed to tease me about the large quantity of food I eat. That's when I grumpily call out, "I get what I can, because no one around here ever feeds me." That's how I land my largest laugh. Because *everyone* knows how much free food I'm fed. Cod, mackerel, mussels, capelin, lobster, salmon, sea trout, redfish, scallops, hare, ptarmigan, partridge berries, blueberries, bear, bakeapples . . . when mainlanders learn how well I'm treated, they often ask what I provide in return. My answer is usually "nothing," but occasionally I tell them that I have helped a few people fill out government forms, taught a man how to read music, written an important letter or two, and given the occasional driving lesson to an older-aged licence-seeker. But I actually believe my greatest contribution to this community is that I validate outport people in a way that the world doesn't.

One McCallum couple had me over for fish-and-brewis, pork scruncheons, fried onions, dried fish, boiled potatoes, and partridgeberry pie. But as good as the company and the cuisine were, what captured my attention was how my hosts packaged up additional dinners and shipped them out to their extended family, before, during, and after our sit-down supper.

I shouldn't have been surprised — I've seen how well this couple's family members treat each other. Many rural Newfoundlanders continue to participate in this long-gone way of life. I've seen how a quartered moose gets divided. How a neighbour will see to it that a couple coming home to a cold house has a hot plate waiting. How a loaf of homemade bread and a jar of jam is always just around the next corner.

The sharing of food in an outport is about seeing that no one goes without. It reminds me of a time in Ontario when I tried to buy some groceries. I say *tried* to buy some groceries because I knew it was a game of chance whether I had enough money to cover my costs. I gambled and lost. The debit machine said my transaction was not approved, and I knew why. I wanted to scream into the microphone — the one the young woman working cash was using to publicly page her boss — that my money shortage was just a result of some sloppy banking that I'd recently (not) done.

I felt humiliated. I wanted to be invisible. At which point the manager arrived. He did an excellent job of making me feel understood, and he worked hard to ease the shame I was experiencing while we arranged an alternative time for me to pay. Yet I still left the store feeling poor, and I wanted everyone to know that I wasn't — like being poor was a crime that I needed to apologize for.

That shame-fuelled agony I experienced got me thinking about those who every day risk being told that they have insufficient funds. I wonder what it feels like to truly be hungry. And I worry about the parent who has to put food back on the shelf, knowing she can't afford it. That's why I tell my Newfoundland neighbours that, whether they're acting on behalf of the less fortunate or simply sharing their blessings, I hope they never stop doing such great and important work. I don't say this because they give any indication that they intend to cease this precious practice. I tell them because they occasionally deserve to have it pointed out to them that they really are wonderful in ways that most of the mainland seldom are anymore.

eleven

What's the difference between a celebrity and a pig? Answer: there are just some things a pig won't do. I learned that joke from Southern Ontario singer-songwriter Fred Eaglesmith and thought it a fitting description of celebrities, because so many stars think so little about self-dignity. But Newfoundlanders are different. Mary Walsh, Shaun Majumder, Rick Mercer — high-profile people highly capable of laughing at themselves and poking fun at others in a respectful way; people who don't give the impression that they would intentionally say or do something stupid just because it might get them on entertainment television.

But there is a second tier of Newfoundland celebrity that most mainlanders have never heard of — artists like actor/author/musician Joel Hynes, comedian Tommy Sexton, and athlete Alex Faulkner. Discovering these talented personalities has enriched my Newfoundland life and taught me much.

I find it fascinating that I can look Faulkner's number up in the Bishop Falls phone book. I find it odd that it's so easy to reach the former professional hockey player, because with every passing day, the possibility of finding celebrities in the phone directory is disappearing. Partly because the majority of public figures carry cell phones, but mostly because we've become such a culture of hero worship that famous people don't feel safe among their fans. It must be worrisome for wealthy athletes to know that every time they go on the road, their schedule is published on the internet and in the newspaper. It wouldn't surprise me if these sports stars had concerns for their family's safety.

Not that Alex Faulkner *starred* in the big leagues. Nor did he play in an era of big contracts. He was, however, the first Newfoundlander to play in the NHL, appearing in one game for the Toronto Maple Leafs in 1961 and another hundred for the Detroit Red Wings, between '62 and '64. He played a very capable support role for some of hockey's all-time greats — Gordie Howe, Bob Baun, and Terry Sawchuk, to name a few. Twice he went to the Stanley Cup Finals, before a broken hand and torn knee ligaments cut his NHL career short. He also played three years with Willie O'Ree in California in the WHL — O'Ree being the first black man to play in the NHL. "Willie was my right winger," Alex tells me. "I used to joke with him that [as his center] I was responsible for putting him on the only All-Star team he ever played on. But Willie was quite a good hockey player and quite a nice guy."

When I ask Alex about the differences between playing for the Gulls in San Diego and fighting off aggressive gulls in Bishop's Falls, he laughs a gentle laugh. "Playing in San Diego was beautiful," he said. "The temperature never dropped below fifty degrees and rarely got over eighty. Plus, I had my whole family down there with me — my wife, Doris, and our two girls and our son. Yes, sir, playing in San Diego was beautiful."

Alex, clearly a considerate man, has a couple of questions for me, wanting to know how a come-from-away ended up in an isolated outport, and asking, "How's it been for you?"

"Just great," I tell him. "These outport people couldn't be treating me better."

"That's Newfoundlanders for you," he says. "The story goes that when they were shooting the movie *The Shipping News*, the lead actor [Kevin Spacey] showed up in Newfoundland with two bodyguards, and he took them with him when he went outside for the first time. But after he'd walked down the street once, he sent his bodyguards home. I guess where he came from, he was worried about being swarmed by fans. But in Newfoundland, a couple of people just said hello to him, and that was all they did. He was surprised by this."

Surprise comes for me when Alex and Doris invite me to lunch. I only phoned hoping to hear a story or two, so being asked to eat with the Faulkner family is a gracious gift. As is the way that Alex greets me at the door to their well-kept Cape Cod home. "Come on in, David. Doris made us food like the kind you're used to eating in Ontario," the still-solidly built senior says, extending a firm hand and wearing a warm, welcoming smile.

It's not hard to see how Doris picked up an understanding of a mainlander's diet — loyally following her husband across the continent while he played for teams in Rochester, Pittsburgh, Cincinnati, Memphis, and San Diego — but it is considerate of her to take into account my cultural background. And it's generous of Alex to open up about his childhood in Bishop's Falls. "My four brothers and I would start the winter playing on Purchase Pond," he says. "It was the first to ice over. A few weeks later, we'd move onto Diamond Pond. Diamond Pond was a little bigger, so it took longer to freeze. Then, when the Exploits River froze, we'd move onto that. But my father always told us that we weren't allowed on the river until the ice was thick enough that the horses and oxen could walk across it on their way to get wood for the mill.

"And, I'll tell you, we listened to Dad. He drove a locomotive for the CNR. Basically, he kept us in gear — a hockey stick cost $1.10 back then — and my mother kept us in grub — homemade beans and molasses buns — so we could just play hockey all winter. There were many mornings when they'd wake up and we'd already be gone, getting in some hockey before we went to school. But my parents weren't trying to produce professional hockey players. They just believed that if we were playing hockey, we weren't getting in trouble. Yes sir, they just believed that pond hockey was a good thing for boys to do before and after school."

I've taught at several Canadian colleges and universities. The highlight of my career came when a student arrived at my office needing to speak with me. I had no idea who this learner was. I had over eight hundred students, and schools like to cram as many as they can into large lecture halls. It makes for a bad education, but it saves money, which is what schools want. Then this young man shows up needing to tell me he is a homosexual and that he lives in student residence where he fears for his safety. He was afraid some fool was going to beat him with a baseball bat. After calming him, the rest was easy — the college made sure his worries were addressed and his studies supported. Today he's got two diplomas and a great job in Florida.

It meant the world to me that I had earned that student's trust. It was heartening to learn that he realized his situation was safe with me, and that I would try to help him with his concerns. But that was 2001, in liberal-thinking Southern Ontario — not seventies and eighties Newfoundland, where the comic Tommy Sexton of *CODCO* was living in an openly gay way during a period of pathetic prejudices.

Born in St. John's in 1957, Sexton, an honours student, quit school in grade ten to pursue an acting career. *CODCO* was a Newfoundland comedy company that began as live theatre called *Cod on a Stick*. Broadcasting on CBC from '87 to '92, *CODCO* starred Sexton, Greg Malone, Cathy Jones, Mary Walsh, and Andy Jones. The show lasted five seasons, for a total of sixty-three episodes.

In 1991, with the Mount Cashel Orphanage child-abuse scandal all over the Newfoundland news, the CBC decided not to air a *CODCO* sketch called "Pleasant Irish Priests in Conversation," in which three Catholic priests discuss their sexual preferences. While *CODCO* continued, some Newfoundlanders considered the CBC's decision not to air the skit a betrayal and a cowardly act that weakened the show.

Following the end of *CODCO*, several cast members went on to create the long-running TV comedy *This Hour Has 22 Minutes*. Sexton wrote a film entitled *Adult Children of Alcoholic Parents: The Musical*.

Adult Children of Alcoholic Parents: The Musical was in production in 1993 when the thirty-six-year-old Sexton died of AIDS-related illnesses. In 2001, Tommy's sister, filmmaker Mary Sexton, produced an honest documentary called *Tommy . . . A family portrait*. The Tommy Sexton Centre — a housing complex for people living with HIV and AIDS — was opened in St. John's in 2006.

I've only just discovered the talents of Tommy Sexton. Now I'm convinced that the people of this province had a creative genius living among them, but that most

Newfoundlanders didn't know this at the time. Yet, looking back at Sexton's colleagues and some of his siblings, I have concluded that Tommy had an admirable support group surrounding him in an era when most gays did not.

Among today's Newfoundland celebrities, Joel Thomas Hynes is my favourite. I love his novels — *Down to the Dirt* and *Right Away Monday*. I smiled when I read, in *Right Away Monday*, Joel's reference to the aforementioned Fred Eaglesmith. Not only because using Fred's remorseful music is a perfect way to set the stage for a down-and-out feller facing a grim situation, but also because you just don't see Fred's name referenced in a whole lot of fiction.

"Yeah, I think Fred and I are kindred spirits," Joel says when I speak with him at his St. John's row house. "We cross paths now and then. I have a lot of respect for his art and his work ethic, and he reads my stuff." But I suspect it's with our mutual admiration of Fred that the things Joel and I have in common begin to end. Because if Joel's writing is any indication of the life he's lived, being raised on the Irish Loop, he's seen an entirely different world than I did growing up in White Bread, Ontario. Joel's books are very much about the devastation to be found in some dreadfully hard homes and in bars like you find in the centre of St. John's — homes ruled by angry parents who find it easier to beat a child than to talk to her. And bars where guys get so bent out of shape that spending a night on the street sleeping in their own urine while their old lady gets it on with her drug dealer in the alley alongside is more familiar than family.

"That's not really what my books are about," Joel insists. "That's just the action — the backdrop — for those characters. Those stories are more about people looking for connection with each other and their place in society. My novels have been dismissed as grungy books, but anybody who thinks that is missing the point. That action makes for great filler, but those books are about people searching for connection.

"As for some of my writing being set in the 'hood, well, I could live somewhere else, but downtown St. John's is the first place where I've ever felt genuine community, so I don't worry about my truck or my home getting broke into. No. Not me. And while I've had offers to go live places where I could maybe achieve more fame and make more money, I don't want that hollow kind of fame, and I'm not just in this for the money.

"Do I like it when my work gets a good review? Yes. And is it nice when I get a cheque in the mail? Of course it is. But if I didn't get those things, this is still the work I'd do. Because this is what I am, and I find it easy to be an artist here. Plus, I've got a nine-year-old son who lives with me part-time. So St. John's is where my priorities are, and Newfoundland is where I feel at ease."

While watching *The Man of a Thousand Songs*, a documentary about Newfoundland singer-songwriter — and Joel's uncle — Ron Hynes, I came away thinking Joel was the film's star. While the senior Hynes is asked to provide insight into the long list of demons he deals with, it is his protégé, Joel, who actually gives viewers what they're wanting. Ron, who has since died as a result of his addiction issues, spends much of the documentary distractingly speaking about himself in the third person. "I think this film is about Ron's . . . dark side," Ron says. "He's definitely the troubled creature and he's the most impatient creature . . . He took over completely. He took over my life, my mind, my heart, my soul, my career . . ."

So it is left to the no-nonsense Joel to courageously speak directly about not only Ron's issues — "He got accepted into this [rehab] program" — but also his own. "Same place I eventually went myself. I ain't no angel," Joel confesses, before insightfully saying, "You know, it is really exhausting, the amount of energy you expend when you attempt to get someone into treatment when you don't understand the exact nature of their addiction."

A shaggy-haired, unshaven, chain-smoking tough guy, Joel is also an incredible communicator, sharing all kinds of heartfelt data about an uncle whom he dearly loved. Despite his rugged roots, I suspect Joel's rebel front is an age-old effort meant to keep himself safe, because in listening to him talk, you realize that Joel Thomas Hynes is not only a tremendously talented artist, but also an extremely clever man who no longer needs a thug persona to survive.

While there is a great deal more about this lovely film that intrigues me, to share such detail could spoil, for viewers, some significant content at the core of this fascinating flick. But know that after watching *The Man of a Thousand Songs* a thousand times — I have my own addictive qualities, truly — I get the feeling that Joel Hynes, unlike so many celebrities, would never intentionally participate in any soul-sucking, dignity-robbing event designed to catch some fan's attention or sell a movie. It's just not who he is or where he comes from.

twelve

It's been said that Flora Feaver (mother of Junior and wife of Clyde) had a minor stroke. Now what in the world is a *minor* stroke? There is nothing minor about the interruption of blood flow to the brain. There is nothing minor about having a stroke in an isolated outport, and there is nothing minor about putting your life in the hands of a province that can't get their act together regarding ferry service.

Not that the men and women who work on Newfoundland's ferries can't be counted on, but the governments responsible for the safe movement of McCallum residents have their own mandate — money. So when Flora concluded that she was suffering a stroke during one of the many times when McCallum's ferry was not in good working order, she knew she was in a difficult situation.

McCallum residents know that calling in a helicopter for an emergency is really not an option they can count on. Government has never actually told us we can't call for a copter, but we can all read between the lines. Outport people intuitively know that fast and efficient helicopter rides are only available to politicians and high-ranking hydro officials and that the loss of an outport person will actually play out well for a government that's determined to scare people out of rural Newfoundland.

So what was Flora to do? Answer: call in the coast guard. Fortunately, the CCGS *Vladykov* was tied up in McCallum's harbour. What are the chances of that? "Best kind," Flora said. "That big boat flew across the bay. She had medical people on her who monitored my heart and measured my blood pressure. If one had to leave me alone, another would take their place. They kept me and Clyde and [my son] Riley comfortable, and they worked to keep me from feeling afraid."

If there's a silver lining in Flora's suffering, it's that her ordeal landed her fifteen minutes of fame on *The Fisheries Broadcast* — North America's longest-running radio program and a lifelong favourite of Flora's — where host Jamie Baker called her his best interview ever. Some lingering loss of feeling in her fingers, however, has interfered with Flora's housework — a task that Clyde and Riley helped pick up the slack with until Clyde needed emergency medical attention too, after falling onboard *his* boat.

The seventy-eight-year-old fisherman said he heard his ribcage crack. Boats can be treacherous when spring conditions create condensation that becomes an ice rink without warning. Boom. Down Clyde went, busting three ribs when he landed on the fibreglass structure that houses his boat's outboard motor.

Good thing the Feavers' guardian angels were at work once again. What if Clyde had been up the bottom of Facheux Bay? As it was, ninety minutes passed between the time a helicopter was called and when it arrived to take him to the hospital. It didn't help that our rescue mission went down in an extremely dangerous environment. The wharf we were working from had been badly beaten down by wind and ice during a recent storm. No one had talked about it, but as we came and went, we all knew our footing could have come out from under us at any time.

That was a stressful hour and a half for a lot of folks. I was impressed with the men who patiently worked with Clyde to not only comfort him, but to accept the fact that his pain was so extreme, he gave every indication he intended to never move again. I realize he was only trying to hold himself together, and he was a gentleman throughout, but Clyde was clearly not cooperating.

"You're going to have to lay down at some point," Clyde's closest caregivers told him.

"No sir. Not going to happen," he firmly replied, holding his upper body as stiff as he could. We would all laugh a nervous laugh until finally, while working to manage the risk of internal bleeding and a punctured lung, Clyde was gently forced onto his back.

A nurse in town for a funeral arrived carrying personal painkillers that Clyde quickly consumed. A short time later, our buddy's sense of humour began to return.

"Are you cold, Clyde?"

"I've been colder," said the man who has spent much of his winter life chasing caribou, hares, and ptarmigan across Newfoundland high country for weeks at a time. And when I asked Clyde — an incredible cook — who was going to feed me in the event he was laid up for a while, he politely pointed out, "I think you're going to lose weight, my son."

Then another amazing characteristic about outport life occurred. It was after the rescue crew stretchered Clyde into a warm building that everyone else went to work. Buns, bread, juice, jam, fruit, cookies, tea . . . everything a person could need seemed to appear out of the sky. Everything except an emergency helicopter.

Clyde's biggest concern? "I'm not going to the hospital in my rubber boots," he said several times, and after an hour of the rest of us ignoring his wishes, he calmly stated, with no shortage of authority, "Now either somebody is going to slip these old boots off me now and get me my good boots, or nobody is going to be lifting me onto no helicopter." To which everyone agreed. It was time to do what we were told.

There are other fine men in McCallum, but Clyde might be the best. Clyde is a sweet blend of hard work, high integrity, abundant skill, and a strong code of admirable behaviour, a difficult standard for his four sons — John, Junior, Glen, and Riley, all of whom remain in McCallum — to measure up to, but a way of living that they've all met head on. More than anything, perhaps, that's what McCallum life has done for me — it has required that I get close to some amazing males, men unlike any I've previously met. Men like Lloyd Durnford — the luthier.

Lloyd looks away when I call him a luthier. A luthier

is someone who repairs and builds stringed instruments — guitars, mandolins, violins. A modest man, Lloyd certainly hasn't tagged himself with that title. After a lifetime of working as a commercial fisherman, I'm sure it isn't easy for Lloyd to say he is something else. Yet, in his new career as a guitar repair person, Lloyd is quickly approaching Malcolm Gladwell's ten-thousand-hour mark — the milestone the best-selling author suggests is a requirement for success, the idea being that people need to practice a task for ten thousand hours if they intend to master it.

These days, becoming a luthier requires learners serve an apprenticeship or study at school, unless, like Lloyd, they live in an isolated outport, where trial and error and searching out information on the internet become their main methods of learning.

Lloyd is always reading about stringed instruments, or talking about them with those who value music as much as he does. A brief chat with Lloyd's supportive woman, Linda, will tell you how many hours he spends surfing, searching the planet for inexpensive parts and damaged instruments. One night, I carried my accordion over to Lloyd and Linda's home in hope of playing the song "Saltwater Joys" with him, only to find that Lloyd's favourite guitar was out of order. After years of wear, it was warping. Then, out of their backroom came a beautiful black six-string that Lloyd had bought online for one dollar because it had a big hole in its body and a damaged internal infrastructure. No way can he fix that, I thought to myself. So imagine my surprise when that guitar suddenly appeared repaired. "It's got a real *sharp* sound," Lloyd said, as he picked away at "The Star-Spangled Banner" in an effort to emphasize each note. Now he's constructing an entire guitar from scratch.

Lloyd sees stringed instruments as pieces of art. He really can't stop creating; he constructs necks, applies polymerized products, even improvises, carving a saddle and nut — the parts that support the strings at each end of the instrument — out of moose antler. It looks as attractive as African ivory, but is as Newfoundland as codfish and capelin.

So unless there is a buyer in McCallum, I imagine it is just a matter of time before Lloyd's restored guitar is back online with a fair-market markup because mainlanders and Newfoundlanders alike are increasingly buying Lloyd's reconditioned instruments. I respect all who can navigate a career change, but anyone short of retirement age who can reinvent themselves in an isolated outport I hold in especially high esteem.

Another man worth watching is Lloyd's good buddy Russ Fudge. I'm not particularly close to Russ myself, but it's easy to see how much he means to the other men in this community — a highly discriminating crowd that will humble you in a heartbeat if you're not acting in the best interest of the whole. Very much a man's man, Russ shows up for darts clean-cut, with a closely cropped beard. Wearing a rugged, full-bodied, green checkered shirt and casual black desert boots against grey jeans and sporting a handsome little pocket-watch, Russ presents an appealing profile. Even the darts he flashes showcase complementary colours. But when I tell him how much I enjoy his fashion sense, he looks at me like I have two heads and firmly informs me that his wife, Sheila, dresses him. At least I think that's what he said. Because, with my grip on the Newfoundland accent so sketchy, I find Russ's Muddy Hole dialect the most difficult to decipher.

Russ is interesting to talk about books with. "I'm not a good reader. I never learned how. But I do like books about the Wild West. Me and the boys on the boat will pass around westerns," the Grand Banks trawler employee explains. "Yes sir, we love our westerns." It's this attraction to all things country and western that intrigues me — how a man living on a part of the continent that couldn't be farther away from where the stories of the Wild West come from could fall in love with the genre.

"I like books and movies about guns," he says. "Rifles and pistols, Lee–Enfields and Smith & Wessons, bolt-action and lever-action, thirty ought sixes . . ." Clearly pleased to share his passion, Russ believes that his interest in all things C&W began in the seventies when outport people started purchasing the noisy generators required to run televisions. "That's when I started watching westerns and war movies. I'd watch westerns like *The Mountain Men,* starring Brian Keith and Charlton Heston. That's my all-time favourite," Russ says of the 1980 classic, in which Keith plays an argumentative trapper who, with his good buddy Heston, wages war with native cultures.

Frequently changing the direction of our dialogue as fast as he cleans fish, Russ now wants to talk about his real-life heroes. "You know, Newfoundland's Bob Bartlett was quite the guy," the proud islander states as he loans me his only copy of Captain Bob's log, a diary documenting Bartlett's forty years of excursions into the arctic, his journey to the North Pole with Robert Peary, and the heroic deeds he accomplished along the way. "Yes sir, that Bob Bartlett was an interesting guy."

No more intriguing than you, Russell. No more compelling than many McCallum men.

thirteen

If you're a fan of adventure, you've probably imagined what it might have been like to participate in some of the world's most celebrated explorations or adventures: Captain Cook's mapping of uncharted territory, Amelia Earhart's groundbreaking crossing of the Atlantic, Edmund Hillary's climbing of Everest, Jeanne Baré's first female circumnavigation of the world, Jacques Cousteau's examination of the Earth's oceans . . .

Of all the adventures that I'm familiar with, the one that resonates the most with me is Meriwether Lewis and William Clark's transcontinental crossing of America to the Pacific Ocean. No doubt my tendency to gravitate towards this overland expedition has a lot to do with my landlubber backstory, because I find it easier to picture myself being part of Lewis and Clark's Corps of Discovery than I do any ocean expedition.

My preference for cross-country adventures is comparable to the way that Newfoundlanders find it easier to identify with Brigus's Bob Bartlett and his ocean explorations than they do, say, someone who walked across Niagara Falls tethered to a tightrope. Taking risks for risk's sake just isn't in the Newfoundlander's DNA. Braving the North Atlantic Ocean, however, in the best interest of your family and friends is. So if there is one ocean-related adventure that I wish I could have been part of, it's the 1965 winter trip to take down, pick up, and bring back from the abandoned isolated outport called Cape La Hune, what today is McCallum's St. Peter's Anglican Church. I'm no church-goer, but to have been part of the planning, preparation, and eventual implementation of this effort to replace McCallum's declining church would have been gratifying for me. To assemble a team of seamen willing to take on that task, arrange for the loan of a local schooner (Wilson Riggs's *Stewart Rose*), and make that windy trek westward on behalf of their friends' and families' wishes to worship their god was, on the part of the participants, brotherly and brave. I would have found that demanding journey with George Wellman, Lloyd Riggs, Hartland Wellman, Clarence Riggs, Hayward Durnford, George Chapman, and George Feaver to be a thrilling experience.

It's true that the relocation of homes and other buildings was, in that era, in Newfoundland, not uncommon — especially for folks forced to resettle. But I see the doers of these tasks as having no less courage and conviction than those today who take risks for far more self-serving reasons like personal praise, publicity, and economic gain.

To only heap approval, however, on born-and-bred Newfoundlanders for their courageous contributions to this island is an act of discrimination — a still surprisingly common occurrence around here. It's been a long time since there has been anyone on this rock whose origins are not from elsewhere. Almost two hundred years have passed since Newfoundland's earliest settlers killed off the island's native Beothuk. So, one way or another, we're *all* visitors to this precious place — a concept that's lost on many of the locals.

I'm always a little taken aback when Newfoundlanders are afraid to admit that their ancestry might include people originally from Portugal or the Basque Country. Or that they're part Mi'kmaq for all they know. Yet it's also disappointing that this resistance regarding their beginnings recently changed somewhat, when the federal government offered money and benefits to Newfoundlanders with native origins. Suddenly those who hated natives most were trying to convince others that they were one.

I of course am thrilled with the idea that there are people from away who have been a positive influence on this province. And it was while searching out these non-Newfoundlanders who have historically contributed to this island's well-being that I found my favourite — the unheralded ninety-two-year-old American Jean Newell — at her Bath, Ontario, home, where I asked her to describe her experience on the Great Northern Peninsula between 1941 and '46.

"I was only twenty-one when I accepted employment as a nurse in St. Anthony, at the Grenfell Mission," the adorable Newell said in such a spirited way that it's impossible not to feel optimistic about aging. "You know how it is when you're twenty-one — everything is an adventure. So when I accepted that nursing position, I didn't know if Newfoundland was on this continent's east coast or west. I just knew I wanted to make a difference in the lives of others.

"Then, a short time after I arrived, a man approached me and said I had to go with him to his outport home. Now remember I grew up in New York City where you're taught at an early age not to go away with a stranger. I thought if I went with him that my poor dear mother would never see me again. Then I realized this man had a very sick child in need of care. So off I went." She swings her arms slightly, in an industrious marching sort of way.

"Newfoundland was the first place I'd seen starvation, mostly because merchants were taking advantage of fishermen, selling them goods in a bartering way that was designed to keep fishermen always in debt, to the point where these workers had to just about give their fish away for free, to a degree where they couldn't afford to feed their families.

"My late husband, Ike [Newell, a teacher from Cupids, Newfoundland], when he realized that these merchants were giving fishermen only three cents per pound for their codfish, took those men into the woods and taught them how to efficiently build boxes to store their fish in, and he showed them how to best use ice off icebergs to keep those fish from spoiling. Then he helped ship that fish to Halifax and North Sydney, where they got twenty-five cents per pound. A lot of people thought that Ike must have been religious because he was so generous, but he was agnostic — he was just an unselfish person.

"While Ike's early education came from a one-room schoolhouse on Conception Bay, it didn't stop him from going on to study at Oxford. Ike's intelligence became clear when he was invited to work with Joey Smallwood at the National Convention to determine what Newfoundland's postwar future needed to look like. That's when we moved to St. John's — from '46 to '48 — where, all of a sudden, Ike's working with famous men like Joey, Bill Keough, Gordon Bradley . . . they were all important contributors to that convention because they turned what was shaping up to be a discussion on constitution into a social debate about the welfare of starving outport people.

"Yes, Joey Smallwood was an egomaniac, talking on about himself and taking credit for everyone else's work, but that doesn't change the fact that he, like Ike and those other men, brought a social conscience to a discussion that had mostly been merchants lobbying for their own economic interests. But now I sound like Joey, talking on and on. Those who read your book are going to get bored when they hear my stories."

No they won't, Jean. Lots of people will be pleased to know of your and Ike's unselfish wartime efforts to assist outport people. Many will see the two of you as adventurers who weren't motivated by fame and fortune, and it's good for Newfoundlanders to know that there have always been a few outsiders who had this island's best interest at heart.

McCallum residents will soon be able to watch an intriguing international-adventure story unfold right in our own harbour, because McCallum is where you'll eventually find the *Evil-Lyn,* a steel thirty-seven-foot sailboat named in honour of an animated actress by its builder Didi Franzmeyer and his partner Marion Jackson. German nationals, Didi and Marion have recently become McCallum's only other come-from-aways. If you think it was hard for *me* to move here, imagine how difficult it is for those who come from another country. As different as my everyday life is, I'm still standing on Canadian soil. Didi and Marion, on the other hand, could be ordered to leave this country at any time.

"Yes, plans for the *Evil-Lyn* were bought in Holland, but Didi built her in our barn in Germany," the spunky middle-aged Marion tells me, her multi-coloured mohawk haircut blowing in the wind. "And right now he has sailed the *Evil-Lyn* as far as the Netherlands." Marion and I are standing in front of the McCallum house that the couple recently purchased as part of their plan to spend the remainder of their lives sailing this province's gorgeous shores, if not from McCallum, which is at risk of resettling, then another cute community.

"I have come to Newfoundland by airplane with our two dogs, while Didi is in Rotterdam making plans to get our boat to North America, and that has not been easy. We are simply trying to get all of us and our boat here safely, without having to spend all our money doing it, but every day we get a new surprise. Hopefully he will be here soon," she says again of her sailor husband, understandably unable to stop talking about him. "Because, right now, it is all very stressful."

With neither member of this gutsy but inexperienced sailing couple feeling comfortable crossing the Atlantic on their own, they've hired a freighter to bring their boat to North America — a business deal that has brought with it some difficulties, including last-second news that the shady freighter hired to bring the *Evil-Lyn* to Rhode Island has suddenly changed their policy about allowing passengers. So Didi will need to temporarily part with the boat that he spent twelve years building and instead fly to Boston, bus to Newport, find ten days' accommodation, and wait for his pride and joy to arrive.

The couple's trust level is understandably low, but if all goes according to plan, Didi and the *Evil-Lyn* will be back on the water shortly, travelling past Massachusetts, Maine, and Nova Scotia before crossing the Gulf of St. Lawrence. "At which point I will be very happy to see him," Marion reminds me.

"I worry about him, because he never gets a chance to sleep, sailing alone. And, while some couples find it difficult to live together on a small boat, that is not the way it is with Didi and me — we are finding it hard to be separated. We're very unhappy to be without each other. So when I see him come sailing into McCallum, I will be the happiest person in the world. Then we will lock ourselves in our house, closing all the curtains, and no one will see us for two weeks."

fourteen

Today's long journey starts with a short ride through the passage that runs between Daniel Island and the Devil's Knob. I'm not surprised that the skipper has us hard to the right in an effort to avoid the underwater rocks that lurk to our left. It's the wee hours of the morning and we're on our way to the deepest region of the Bay Despair — fifty kilometres inland, as wild a landscape as Canada has to offer. Big hills, deep valleys, large rocks, and abundant beauty. We're hoping to see some moose, but right now it's only blackness and trickery. Lucky for us there is little wind, so the water is somewhat smooth. Yet, travelling in an open boat the way we are, we generate our own chill factor.

I'm baffled by the bright light that unexpectedly appears when we turn towards Buffett Tickle, when a big number of bulbs come blinking and flashing at us from one of the salmon cages that are increasingly showing up everywhere. It's not that I don't understand how lights are needed for navigation given the enormous territory that a cage covers, but seeing this much light pollution on a wilderness journey seems sad and unnecessary. Especially when it causes me to lose sight of a handsome sky.

While I'm the only member of this crew moaning and complaining about this invasive event, I know I'm not alone in disliking it. I can see it in the others' expressions — they're as agitated as I am. Light caroming off of cliffs at this time of the morning is an insensitive reminder that the feelings of the people who live on these waters are an afterthought. Nobody gives a damn about us or that one of Newfoundland's few remaining fisheries is at further risk because no one in power cares enough to consider the precautionary principle — the idea that if you're unsure about the environmental impact that fish farming has on the ocean, you proceed with caution.

The only thing that matters to the province of Newfoundland and Labrador is the wants and needs of politicians and big business — a bunch of like-minded individuals and organizations that I increasingly find impossible to tell apart, who would pull the last wild creature from the sea if they thought they could make a penny from it, and who are not particularly smart when it comes to seeing beyond the almighty dollar. Don't get me wrong, there are some clever people involved in politics and big business, but they're not as smart as they think they are, rendering them the most dangerous kind of decision-maker. They'll tell you that they are creating employment — like the jobs they provide should make you want to get down on your knees for them — but are you aware of the conditions and terms by which aquaculture employees work? Low hourly pay, ridiculously long days, and no time off for most of the year.

How long can a person work under those circumstances before sickness sets in? And how often in such a high-risk ocean environment can one person work alone before the grim reaper comes calling? I'm sure actuaries have answered these questions, but they've done so on behalf of governments and big businesses that require insurance policies to protect their millions, not the poor working stiff who faces danger daily.

The big questions around here are: What happens to the aquaculture industry when government subsidies dry up? And who can we expect to pick up the pieces when businessmen walk away with their pockets lined, laughing? Because fish farming shows no indication that it will ever find success on its own, especially if it's required to be environmentally responsible. In the meantime, government shows little sign it will ever learn to do its work differently.

My best learning occurs when I'm taught content that explains and reinforces ideas that I already naturally knew — like a college course I once took on critical thinking. That curriculum gave me permission to feel comfortable about things that I thought might be right but had doubts about until someone scholarly validated what I intuitively knew to be true.

Of course, not all education comes from courses. Practical experience is priceless, and reading has played a large role in my learning — especially *book* reading. Three in particular: John Steinbeck's *Grapes of Wrath*, Michael Lewis's *Moneyball*, and Edward Abbey's *Desert Solitaire* — *Grapes of Wrath* because it opened my eyes to the plight of the oppressed, *Moneyball* because it inspired me to look at the world in ways it's seldom seen, and *Desert Solitaire* because the content really resonated with me. Abbey was the first author to capture my attention as I entered adult-hood, because he was angry and he knew why. Thirty-one years my senior and ecologically ahead of his time, Ed filled a vacant hole in my heart, in an area of expertise that I was aching for information on, in an era when environmental-ists were seen as alarmists. As if.

Sensitive to the disappearance of wilderness, Ed's base was the American Southwest, but it could have been any-where. It could have been Newfoundland, where, if you consider the commonly accepted definition of wilderness as "five thousand continuous acres of roadless area," there is much less wilderness left than the average person realizes, what with the large number of ATVs running around.

Dirt roads are everywhere and getting wider. Newfoundlanders adore their dirt roads, so this develop-ment will only get worse, because the people empowered to protect us against sprawl — our governments — are benefit-ting from such unruly expansion. Unregulated roads make it easier for governments to justify additional development, sell adjacent land, and collect related taxes. Especially when wilderness is no longer pristine enough to warrant protec-tion, in the eyes of policymakers.

Abbey knew this. A student of anarchy, Ed saw politicians as people to keep yourself safe from. "A patriot must always be ready to defend his country against his government," he said, in ways that resulted in government putting Ed on their watch list because he was seen as someone who encouraged ecoterrorism when he wrote about pulling up survey stakes, sabotaging construction equipment, and blowing up dams.

As with many ecological inquiries, I can find no easy answer as to how I feel about this gang who goes to such drastic measures to defend life on Earth. I see the world they work with, and it's a nasty one. On one side of our current socioeconomic scale are the extreme narcissists — unethical people who don't care who or what they kill, as long as they're making money and feeding their ego. So I'm not surprised that, in opposition to this despicable bunch who care about no one but themselves, we find strongly principled activists who are willing to take enormous risks in support of their environmental beliefs, to offset the evil at the other end. I'm not surprised that there are these people who take action on behalf of the planet even when their institutions declare them criminal. Because, in many people's minds, the legality of a law does not alter the fact that that law might be immoral. So while I don't have the conviction, myself, to take such extreme action, I'm no less intrigued that such committed radicals are out there and that I've had a chance to sit with some of them. I'm speaking about Snook and Lucy Lee.

For Snook and Lucy, life on Bonne Bay isn't what it once was. Not only have they both unexpectedly lost their mothers recently, they have not untied their boat from its mooring in more than a month. They haven't felt motivated to get out on the water, not even for a brief boil-up — a cuppa tea, a tin of wieners, and a fistful of jam jams — much less to set a few snares, drag for scallops, and see how their cabin is holding up against winter weather.

Overnighting in that wilderness retreat is no longer as pleasurable for the Lees as it once was, and, while they aren't always open about what they're affected by, both know exactly why they're finding it hard to have fun. What with the number of new aquaculture cages that have been installed alongside their little piece of paradise, it's been difficult for them to relax. They know how the buildup of fish feces on the bottom of the bay is affecting the local lobster ecology. They see the industrial garbage increasingly collecting everywhere, the steady stream of noisy boats, and the way that their favourite trees have been cut down for firewood by aquaculture employees who do their personal work on company time — with highly effective industrial equipment — when no one is watching. Plus, the Lees heard that two months ago, one hundred thousand lice-infected, medicine-saturated salmon escaped from a nearby cage after it was damaged during an extremely violent storm. And even if that estimate is only half-right, Snook and Lucy wonder why no one has made a public announcement, given the environmental importance of such an event. "I just don't see how aquaculture companies get away with things a fisherman don't," Snook says. "Queerest thing, don't you think? If I do something to the land and sea, [the authorities will] take away my boat, my licence, my gear . . . then they give me a big fat fine and put my name in the newspaper."

That's the way it is for many who live on Newfoundland's Southwest Coast. They're miserable about something or somebody — an increase in seal population, a loss in essential services, the selfish actions of politicians like Darin King and Clyde Jackman . . . yet, there's another side to this group. There's a part in their heart that persistently tells them that they continue to live along a gorgeous shoreline, in a great harbour, on a beautiful bay belonging to the most wonderful island in the world. And they know that no matter what outside influences are at work to destroy their way of life, this place they call home is still worth fighting for. That's why Snook and Lucy snuck out last Sunday to sabotage an aquaculture cage.

Surprised? You shouldn't be. The Southwest Coast is a lot of things, including quite contemporary at times.

McCallum folks really do know what needs to happen if they hope to cope. I remember one occasion when four artists paid a winter visit to this isolated outport. Travelling teachers, they were. Non-creatives have gutted the school system's art programs so badly that the only way for a learner to get a balanced education is for the schools to ask touring artists to periodically deliver workshops. Poets, painters, dancers . . . the children love it. I do too. Especially one time, when a St. John's troupe of four got snowed and winded in. It gave me a few additional days of culture and attention that I never would have received otherwise. It didn't hurt that three of the stranded were women.

As the days those artists were marooned in McCallum added up, that group asked if I could get them some authentic outport grub — moose and scallops mostly. Of course, one of my food sources came through once again, and it was no surprise to me that he wouldn't take any money in return for his product. So I took it upon myself to suggest this band of travelling teachers give him a small bag of marijuana — a gift that delighted their grocer. As an abstainer, I found this exchange funny because in the wildest corners of my imagination, the last thing I ever thought I would do in McCallum is find myself in the middle of a drug deal.

fifteen

I'm convinced that there are no Newfoundlanders who aren't aware of the controversial resettlement programs that governments implemented from 1954 to 1974, when thirty thousand people were forced to leave their homes. Even the smallest of schoolchildren today are taught about that time when community services were reduced and neglected — abandoned even — because governments wanted to centralize populations.

When Newfoundland joined Canada in 1949, the Southwest Coast consisted of eighty outports. Nine years later, only thirty-eight remained. McCallum almost passed away as well, when a government study at the time said the outport was doomed to die in ten years and offered residents relocation money in response to this research — an offer that McCallum turned down. As a result of the community's refusal to relocate, many being pressured to leave other outports took shelter in McCallum as the community became a safe haven for those who didn't want to stop living the life.

Given the rural Newfoundlander's oral tradition of sharing resettlement sorrow, knowledge regarding the trauma that resulted from such insensitive programs has been kept alive for a long time. But with ongoing urbanization, and the townies' lack of interest in travelling outside of St. John's, the hundreds of communities that were so hard-heartedly discarded have gradually been forgotten. Communities like Pass Island — a dark, mysterious landmark that sits only 250 metres offshore from the Hermitage Peninsula where it can easily be seen on the horizon when looking south from McCallum.

Because of its nearness to some noteworthy Fortune Bay fishing banks and its proximity to St. Pierre's important political and navigational position, Pass Island was one of the

Southwest Coast's first settled sites. Captain Cook reported that several English fishermen used the island in the summer of 1763 and that two families spent that winter on-site.

By 1836, 56 people called Pass Island home. That citizenry grew to be 110 by 1857, and 215 by 1874, after an Anglican church was built in 1869 and a school a short time after that. With such a solid foundation in place, the next century went as planned for the people of Pass Island. Then a road was built from Seal Cove to Pass Island Tickle, and people predicted that Pass Island's future would be brighter than ever because the community was suddenly only 250 metres offshore from an economically supportive throughway. But when their nearest neighbour, Grole, opted to relocate, isolation anxiety began to set in for the people of Pass Island. For many, this angst was too much for them to take, and Pass Island's population shrunk to 160 by the summer of 1974.

At this point, politicians stepped up resettlement pressure. So when nearby Hermitage built a new fish-processing plant, and modern longliners provided fishermen the opportunity to travel to and from familiar waters, the forces to relocate got to be too great, and Pass Island became the last community to fall to that era's resettlement program, like the last soldier to die in a dubious war. Yet the pride of some Pass Island people was so powerful that, for twenty years afterward, they continued to maintain the town's wharves. If only those Pass Islanders could have held on for one more summer, they would probably still be there, because if the community had survived, a causeway would surely have been built across that 250-metre passage today, and that extended road access would have guaranteed survival of some sort.

I hope to visit Pass Island one day, just to look around. Perhaps I'll search out their cemetery, try to determine where the old buildings sat, and imagine the lives of those who called that community home. Maybe one of my McCallum buddies will run us across on a calm day. I'll offer to pay for fuel, at least. In the meantime, for me and many other McCallum residents, Pass Island will simply remain a monument to some of the sadness that resulted from resettlement.

Of course, many left their outport without a push or a penny. Men like Alex King, who was born in Bradley's Cove in 1922 but died in Erin Mills, Ontario, in 2011, at the age of eighty-eight. While no one remembers exactly when the young Alex left Newfoundland, they know that after he did, he seldom returned. Not that he didn't wish to revisit his childhood home, but he had responsibilities in Ontario, including raising — along with Olive Peddle of Bristol's Hope — seven children.

"He only went back to visit three times over sixty years," his son Dwight tells me when I catch up with him at his Kitchener home. "But my dad had fond memories of Newfoundland. He especially enjoyed building Gander Airport before, and during, World War Two. At one point, my dad wanted to move home to Newfoundland. But my mom didn't. And by the time she died, he believed he was too old to go home. He was afraid rural Newfoundland might be too isolated for an aging person. Plus, everybody was here by then, including great-grandchildren."

Alex's most productive employment came from Canada Packers — today Maple Leaf Foods — in Toronto. "By a Newfoundlander's way of thinking, my dad had the perfect job for a father of seven, given the large amount of food he had access to," Dwight tells me, clearly feeling nostalgic to be talking about his father this way. "Employees got some good discounted cost benefits. You name it, my dad brought it home. Half a pig even. Pay was decent as well, and the guy worked a lot of overtime, shipping stuff to Japan and Europe. I remember him working Saturdays and often more. He worked like crazy, all the time. Obviously, providing for the rest of us was his number one priority. Even when he was slowed by physical ailments — stomach ulcers, prostate cancer, hernias — none of it stopped him from being a worker and a provider."

I ask Dwight what he thinks of his own Newfoundland bloodline. "No doubt I feel some pride around it," he says. "I mean, it's a great province. You can feel the history when you visit it. Especially since [wife] Cathy and I retraced a lot of it when we visited three years ago. While it's all different now, I still felt what it might have been like when my dad was young. His brother Lloyd is still there. He's the last of the brothers still alive. He drove a road grader. And Ralph was a builder — houses, boats — and he fished. I say this because my dad and his brothers were all part of that family's strong work ethic. Even *their* father — my grandfather John — worked in what they called the Boston States for a while. So I suspect my dad's dad planted a seed in such a way that my father grew up knowing he might have to travel a long way for work."

I'm miles from McCallum. I couldn't be much further and still be in Canada. I'm writing from the road — Jewel

Lake, to be exact, an expired gold-mining town in British Columbia's Kootenay mountain range, where I'm visiting with old-time Toronto Maple Leaf Jim Harrison, whom I've also written a book about. The good news is that this is the last stop on my cross-country trip, a journey that began six weeks ago when I boarded the *Marine Voyageur* in McCallum and travelled to Burgeo — a tour that took me to the isolated outports of Francois, Grey River, and Ramea before I proceeded by bus to Deer Lake and then on to Ontario by airplane.

I went to Kitchener to take care of my sister's dogs while she travelled China. From B.C. I'll head east again. I'm going back to Kitchener-Waterloo to tie up some loose ends with friends, but after a brief time in the twin cities, I'll be making my way back to McCallum, the place that I'm presently missing most. That's the mess I'm in — when I'm in Newfoundland I long for my Ontario family and friends, and when in Ontario, I miss McCallum.

Not that my westward push hasn't been pleasurable — quite the opposite actually. I've spent quality time with a lot of good people. It feels right to support my youngest nephew in his pursuit of employment with the Royal Canadian Navy, and it brings me great pleasure to play with my little nieces, ages five and nine. It's also wonderful to celebrate my birthday with people with whom I haven't done so in fourteen years, and it is fun to attend a Blue Jays game.

I enjoy shopping in stores unlike any in Newfoundland. And it is always a treat to spend time with a couple in Kelowna for whom I was best man in 1987. Yet I miss my McCallum friends. I miss the way they sound — the way they smile, laugh, and truly talk differently than the rest of Canada. I miss their kindness. I miss Reg Fudge and am saddened that I will not be there for his eightieth birthday.

I miss Feaver food, Fudge love, Crant and Carter charisma, boardwalk talk with the Wellmans, lovely Durnford deeds, Simms synergy, Skinner skills, sweet Poole and Piercey people, rowdy Riggs, Chapman chatter, and MacDonalds of all kinds — the people, not the restaurant. I even long for Guy Nash's nagging about his horrible hockey team. I miss all the camaraderie and support I receive from the seamen who serve on the ferries. I miss sunrise boat rides and crazy times at the community centre. I crave mussels and moose, and I miss the million-dollar view from my home-office window.

Yet when anyone returns to McCallum after a lengthy time away, they know that there might be an unpleasant surprise waiting for them. House upkeep can be hard. I've seen how salt water and wind can destroy a new doorknob in less than a year. And pipes can be problematic. This is especially true in winter when plumbing you thought you drained freezes solid, because a granite underlay doesn't allow for public water systems to be sunk in soil.

Winds are the worst around here. I've had them twist my entire torso against my will, and that's not a safe feeling. I walk a stretch of boardwalk where there are no lights, so sometimes it's dark. Really dark. "I'm fine," I tell myself, as I scurry towards my house. There are evenings where I wonder, if this blow throws me overboard, how long will I lay on those rocks before someone notices I'm gone, or the tide comes in and takes me away? It isn't that I can't manage. I'm a heavy, strong guy, reasonably steady on my feet anywhere but landwash or on the gunnels of a boat. It's just that some days, the winds are exceptionally threatening.

That's what everyone in McCallum was talking about when Carol and I first asked what winter was like on the Southwest Coast. "The wind . . ." they would say, shaking their head and trying to stifle a nervous smile as they delivered the news. "Oh, my dear, the wind is fierce." But until I experienced it, I really couldn't imagine what it was like. It's hard to comprehend how you could send ten men with heavy sledgehammers under your home, and they couldn't do more than shake your floor for a few minutes, but the almighty wind can torque your entire house every twenty seconds or so, for thirty-six hours straight. That's the part — the duration of the pounding — that wears me out.

I came here for adventure, so I'm mostly practical when a storm arrives. Is everything tied down? Do I have enough firewood to last a couple of days? Because when the wind comes, it comes and comes and comes. It sounds like I am living on the tarmac at Pearson International. The second night is often worse than the first. Even after the storm subsides, conditions are still wild. Everything just seems better because the thumping isn't as sizeable as it has been.

Days later I still feel beat down from it all. Not that it isn't wonderful to witness — to help pull boats ashore in advance of a storm, to feel the anticipation in the air, to see, through salt-encrusted windows, whitecaps roar in to shore in a sheltered harbour, and to hear seasoned seamen say that with every passing decade, wind speed is clearly increasing. And, son of a gun, they say it — over and over and over. The wind is the most talked about subject in all the outports.

When I first moved to McCallum, the ultrahigh humidity caught me by surprise. I find that if you drain an Ontario pipe at the end of August and leave it exposed to open air, you can assume that whatever water you've left lying in low areas will evaporate before real cold arrives. This is not so in an area as moisture-rich as coastal Newfoundland, where

I'm convinced that if you walk away from a drop of water on your kitchen counter at bedtime, that bead will be bigger by morning, after damp air collects in the cool night. Even blasting air pressure through my pipes before leaving town doesn't entirely clear them, given the inefficiencies and inadequacies of do-it-yourself plumbing processes. So the first thing I attempt to do upon returning home after a winter absence is open the tap that brings town water into my house. I say I *attempt* to turn that tap because for more than half a year, it's not uncommon to find my faucet frozen, at which point I plug in some strategically placed heat tape and wait for the technology to take. That's the easy part. It's when that water main is clear that the real work begins — it's not until there is a steady flow of fluid that I notice which pipe connections have been pushed apart by expanding ice.

Only after all plumbing is repaired can I put my life in order after what has always been several days of travel. Not that I ever face these household maintenance challenges alone. My McCallum friends are always there to offer temporary housing and anything else I need. But while I'm grateful for my neighbours' goodness, there is something about stubborn human pride that pushes me to do all the work I can by myself with a goal, at the end of the day crawling into my own bed knowing that I've got my immediate concerns under control. Yet, that's often when the biggest surprise arrives. One time, two minutes after thinking I had everything in order, I heard a loud sound and soon realized my hot-water tank had sprung a large leak. And that no matter how quickly my Hermitage hardware store got me a new tank, stormy seas would delay the ferry from delivering it.

At no point, however, do I wonder if I've got a knowledgeable person to help with tank installation tasks. Any unknowns about assistance become crystal clear when I arrive home to find Lloyd Durnford waiting with a sled to help pull my bags across snowy boardwalks. He has also preheated my house, and his wife, Linda, has seen to it that a pot of moose soup is simmering on my stove.

sixteen

It's hard to know what to say to someone who has amyotrophic lateral sclerosis, or Lou Gehrig's Disease, as ALS is called in parts of the world where people know about baseball's New York Yankee captain who died from the illness in 1941. ALS causes the muscles we normally move voluntarily to gradually break down, weaken, and waste away. Those afflicted have difficulty speaking and swallowing, until gradually they become disabled and highly susceptible to infections, particularly pneumonia. But that's not the worst part — it's that this gradual paralysis occurs while the patient remains mentally alert, rendering the sufferer a prisoner in their own body. That's the horrific situation that McCallum's Margaret MacDonald — a woman of considerable creative talent and entrepreneurial spirit — was in, at fifty-two years of age. And that's the circumstance she so bravely spoke with me about at the St. John's group home that provided her with care through the final stages of her life.

"It might have been better to stay in McCallum for [husband] Terry's job," she says, her speech slurring slightly, a symptom of her sickness. "But I couldn't stay there. When you can hardly walk, and you live on a steep hill in a small house that's not set up for somebody who's got Lou Gehrig's Disease, you have to go someplace where you can get some help. Like when you can't get on and off the ferry without using a stretcher and all the men you need to carry it. Even when [McCallum residents] Anna [Simms] and Barbara [Durnford] would come up the house to look after me . . . how can they be expected to lift me all the time? My right arm and leg don't work, I can't walk, I need a wheelchair, and now my left side is getting weak.

"And I cry all the time," she adds, in reference to her

tendency to weep at unexpected moments, another symptom of the disease as well as the circumstance.

Originally from the Avalon Peninsula's Point La Haye region, Margaret moved to McCallum as a mail-order bride after writing to Terry, a fisherman and McCallum's ministerial layperson. I ask how *he* is doing. "He's understandably upset," she says. "He's got bad nerves. He tells me he doesn't know how he's going to get along without me. But he's here every day, and he feeds me — that's when we talk about things. Like what I want done when I can't breathe no more, because I don't want life support."

Margaret's passing was a highly significant McCallum occurrence, not just because she was friend or family to so many on the Southwest Coast. Nor was Margaret's demise only noteworthy because it represented the loss of a citizen who actively supported many essential services. Margaret's death was of even greater consequence to McCallum because no one in this close-knit community got to avoid watching her horrible disease conduct its deadly business.

We all saw Margaret's earliest symptoms and wondered if they could be corrected — if they were simply her body's response to the drugs she took as part of her lifelong fight against serious arthritis. We wanted to believe that her illness could be managed by those closest to her. But we soon saw that as wishful thinking when her condition escalated into something requiring two home care workers and outside support from St. John's.

We saw how it took more than ten men in total to get Margaret on a stretcher from her home to the ferry and onto a waiting ambulance at the other end when she required further medical attention. And, while it's funny now, we all heard about it, over and over, because Margaret didn't suffer silently — a characteristic that, at the time, was difficult for listeners to bear but, in hindsight, was a warning horn in the fog. It's now easy to see that, before her disease was diagnosed by doctors, Margaret knew something was seriously wrong and was crying out for help.

So while Lou Gehrig's Disease is obviously most painful for the one who has it and those within their immediate circle of support, it is important to acknowledge that, in a tiny outport, it is an excruciating test for everyone when we have to witness serious sickness. It's difficult to watch from such a short distance away, when a strong woman like Margaret MacDonald is so savagely beaten down over the homestretch.

It's also worth noting that Margaret's battle with Lou Gehrig's Disease is not the only tragedy that her McCallum family has faced. There have been others, including a significant rockslide. But it's impossible to comment on that 1981 McCallum occurrence that almost put an end to the MacDonalds' outport presence forever without first honouring a major 1973 landslide that swept four homes into the ocean in nearby Harbour Breton, killing four young children from the same family.

"You're right," Liz MacDonald says. "Our rockslide was a big thing for we McCallum people, but I don't want to sound like we suffered like those poor people in Harbour Breton did." Liz gently adjusts the angle of her cane. Slowed by hip ailments, her ambitious eyes defy her uncooperative body. "There's no comparing what happened to us, down cove, to what happened when those four young Hickey children got killed in Harbour Breton."

MacDonald was a courageous commercial fisher for much of her life, yet the thought of what she's seen is a lot for the sensitive seafarer to think about. So I give her a chance to collect herself before I ask what unfolded when an untold number of rocks fell from a McCallum cliff, destroying one home and forcing four others to relocate to safer ground.

"Four homes had families in them," she clarifies. "They belonged to a father and three of his sons, and another was being built new at the time by a grandson. That's the one that the rocks beat down the worst — the one that was being built new. A stage [a dock] got beat down too. Then people went up in a helicopter to take a closer look at the hill, and they said it wasn't safe for us to stay down cove, so we all resettled someplace different. [George and I and our children] went on road [another McCallum location]. Henry and them moved into the house he's still in behind hydro, but all the others left town. And that's a good thing, because more rocks came down after."

It's when I ask Liz if she recalls her feelings from that fateful day — when a mass of granite came thundering down around her home — that she gives me her most hearty response. "Oh yes, that's what I do," she says, with considerable sadness in her voice and a bit of moisture in her eyes. I learn later that such memories trigger all kinds of thoughts for the MacDonald matriarch, from the events of that scary day in '81 to the loss of George in '96 when he choked on his chewing tobacco. "Oh yes — that's what I do.

"But that was a much more terrible accident in Harbour Breton," she repeats. "We were so lucky, thank God, that none of us got hurt. It could have been much worse for everyone living down cove. Just think about it. There were five families — a father, three sons, a daughter, a grandson, the sons' wives, and fourteen children between them. Look at that big pile of rocks out there now, David, just past Roland's stage, and just think what could have happened."

Geography, genetics, the weather, government . . . they all conspire to make life hard around here. But no matter how much I criticize Newfoundland's authorities for their anti-quated qualities, I have to say that government's ineptness is *nothing* compared to that of the province's churches, where they operate in ways resembling early human history. Like the summer of 2011, when the Anglican Church stripped McCallum's lay reader, Terry MacDonald, of all minister-like privileges because he took a common-law partner after his wife, Margaret, died from Lou Gehrig's Disease.

I imagine Terry was not surprised by the church's choices. Few of us reach midlife without realizing that all kinds of organizations, and many of the people employed to manage them, care more about themselves and their beloved *rules* than they do those who pay their way. So these paragraphs are not about Terry's loss or the church's archaic ruling. This passage is about those who pass pious judgement and how their actions demonstrate how little they understand that their institutional survival is dependent on them regaining relevancy in the lives of their declining clientele.

Like when the local bishop said in a newspaper report that he did not intend to make a public statement regarding MacDonald's defrocking. Why not? Aren't we all aware that people in powerful clerical positions are required to be transparent and accountable? Doesn't everyone know that religious institutions have for centuries betrayed our trust via acts of child molestation and gross error in judgement as it applies to native persons and people of different — or perhaps not so different — sexual orientation? Or are church champions just so ignorant, arrogant, and self-serving that they cover their own needs ahead of those within their diocese? Not that I believe that most people want, when the going gets tough, to turn and run and hide behind outdated "no comment" comments, but that such unwillingness to work for the majority makes the empowered appear cowardly.

Whatever the reasons behind the bishop's failure to be accountable for the stripping of MacDonald's ministerial status, the outports have many questions that need to be addressed. Like, with so many unnerving events occurring in the communities on death row these days, how do church decision-makers see their isolated members' futures unfolding? And how will these events affect the community's efforts to access their god? Questions that anybody in a position of power today should know they have an ongoing responsibility to respond to. Or are the answers to these inquiries also secret?

She doesn't want to answer the phone. It's probably her father and, if it is, she expects he will be angry again. Not angry with her, but she has trouble listening to him rant these days. Last time he phoned he was mad at the man who sells him lumber. "I've bought things from that guy for thirty-three years," he reminds her. "Yet every time I need two-by-fours, they put the most cracked and crooked on the truck and take them to the ferry. I should ship them back but I don't, and they know that."

It's springtime — a time of hope — but things have not gone well for him. Things have not gone well for her either. What with her mom dying, her life has been turned on its head, and her schooling has suffered badly. She feels a lot of shame and guilt for not answering the phone, but she doesn't believe she has it in her to tolerate his talk tonight. It's the final week of her second semester at university, and she still needs to write two exams and finish an assignment that she has already received an extension on.

She's also out of money, and the school's food bank is running low. The student loan she is hoping to receive from government for spring and summer studies won't be in until the end of May, and even then she won't qualify for it if she doesn't attain the academic success they insist upon — scholastic achievement that has always come easy for her but is no longer a guarantee, it seems. Plus, the school counsellor who has given her so much support working through these matters has closed her office until the fall. And no way is she going to ask for financial help from home.

"Funny thing though, about this work I am doing," she whispers to herself. "People can build bridges, boats, or tall buildings, and others will make them famous for their work. But if somebody puts the same effort into their hurting heart, not only will no one tell them they are a hero, some fool will say that person has a mental health problem.

"There really isn't enough time [to be thinking about such sensitive things], though," she adds, agitated. The wealthy owner of the fish-and-chip shop where she works part-time is pestering her to put in more hours. It isn't all the married, father-of-three asshole is pressuring her to do, but she insists that isn't part of her pain. "Enough of this craziness!" she screams to no one, when she's once again overwhelmed with thoughts about the disease that stole her mother from her. "I've got work to do," she says, "and all the worry in the world isn't going to help me get ready for tomorrow morning's exam."

She picks up the phone. "Hello? Oh, hi Father. How are you? Good. Oh, I'm okay, still busy with school, you know, but looking forward to coming home for a short break. I hope the ferry is back [from refit] by then. What's that? Yeah, I know you do, Dad. I miss her too."

seventeen

The children who grew up next door to my McCallum home have recently moved to St. John's. The oldest went to university, and his sister followed a year later to make her way in the work world. This pattern is not unique to McCallum, of course. Families throughout rural Newfoundland experience similar movement among their offspring. But it is especially difficult watching your loved ones leave on a boat the way that outport people have to. Something excruciatingly painful happens when that boat breaks away from the wharf, and you're left staring at a young, forlorn face disappearing into the fog. That's if you're even still standing there. Most McCallum people will head back to the house before that unpleasant experience can occur, while others won't come down to the water at all.

Yet the entire community prepares these kids for their exit. "Unless you want to fish, and you've shown no signs of that," they are often told, as everyone gets them ready for the inevitable, "there isn't anything for you here once you're done school." Uncles, aunts, parents . . . they all say, "No, my dear — one day you'll have to leave McCallum for the city. St. John's, Halifax . . . or maybe you'll go farther, to Toronto or Calgary." Words that slash and tear at a parent's heart when they have to make such a statement.

"It is a terrible thing to have to see your children leave," the forty-year-old fish-farming father of the two young people who previously lived next door to me says. He and I are sharing in the shovelling of snow off the boardwalk that runs between our homes. "I know it's normal," he adds, casting his eyes away so I can't catch him crying. "I want them to go out and find their way. But I'd be lying if I said it doesn't kill me that they're not here.

"We took the bus into St. John's to check on them a few weeks ago. They're doing good. My boy is doing a good job at school, he's got a girlfriend, and he knows how to manage his money — better than his father does, that's for sure," my friend jokes, trying to find humour in an emotionally awkward situation. "We still do our best to help them out — like pay their phone bills, so you know they can call if they need to. But, really, the boy's doing a good job at school and managing his money.

"Our daughter is doing pretty good too. She's had no problem getting jobs, and when they're not what she wants — say the hours aren't good, or if her job is too far from where she lives — she goes and gets a new one. She's got an apartment and a roommate, she pays her rent, and she's still got a little left over every month for shopping. Yes sir, the girl loves to shop. So while I'm afraid to think of my little girl going downtown, it does make me happy to think of her buying another pair of cheap earrings at the Avalon Mall." Then he looks away again, this conversation clearly killing him.

I've seen where a youngster destined for college or university leaves on Labour Day, still possessing considerable childlike characteristics, only to return at Christmas as an adult. Like Hermitage's Trent Hollett, for example, Hermitage being the tiny town where our ferry takes us, McCallum's gateway to the world.

Trent left home thinking like a high school student who

hails from a town of four hundred people and came back for the holidays an independent-thinking soul who had successfully completed a semester at the College of the North Atlantic's St. John's campus in the school's popular paramedic program.

Not that I know Trent well, but I have seen him hanging around his mom's store. Mostly behind the snack bar, digging in at dinner when help is needed or filling his own face. While I always thought Trent to be a clever, respectful kid, he was still, understandably, very much a mother's son. So when I spoke with the eighteen-year-old about his first semester at college, I wasn't convinced he was the same guy. His voice sounded the same, but the words he used and the manner in which he delivered them were much more mature than I remembered. That's what fourteen weeks in an intensive program, in a mid-sized city, far from everything you've ever known, can do for a young man or woman — enough so that I had to tease Trent about the changes in him that happened while he was away.

"It *was* a big adjustment," he admits. "I'm not just talking about the schoolwork either. I mean, it is a difficult program. Every day they give us more and more information that we need to take in, but the most challenging part for me was leaving home.

"Living with my dad helps a lot. Right from the start, knowing where I was going and who I was going to be with [was] always better than not knowing. But it's still not the same as living in my Hermitage home, in the town I was raised in, eating my mom's home-cooked meals. And there is a lot of support here [in Hermitage]. Even now, when I walk around town, my old teachers want to know how college is going for me. Plus, I wasn't the only kid from here who had to leave home and work hard. I've got friends studying nursing, business administration, taking university entrance courses, buddies from Hermitage, Sandyville, and Seal Cove.

"Just getting around St. John's can be tough. Plus, my dad doesn't actually live in St. John's — he's in CBS [Conception Bay South], so that means a twenty- to thirty-minute drive to school every day. And I say twenty to thirty minutes, but that's only if weather is good, when sometimes it isn't. No sir, winter driving is not good some days. You've got to take it slow if you want to stay safe." I smile. Trent sounds more like the common-sensed young man who came home from paramedics' college than the schoolboy who went away.

Soon another learner will be leaving. A McCallum girl. The whole town feels heavy in anticipation. You can already see the pain on her mother's face. Her grandparents are showing some wear and tear too. Since she was a baby, she's run in and out of their home more often than anyone can count. Her little brother is also carrying a large load regarding her approaching departure, and her friends are experiencing considerable sadness. Yet the young woman who is leaving will be fine. I hear she wants to be a teacher. She's certainly had some good ones to learn from, and she knows how to work today's technology, what with online education being such a big part of today's outport programs. Plus, her parents have made a point of getting her and her brother in and out of the city for everything from swimming lessons to carrying on with their cousins, so her adjustment to townie life won't be as big as it might have been had she stuck close to home.

I'm not sure how they plan to get her into St. John's for her fast-approaching first day. Her dad is currently catching redfish on the Grand Banks — 250 kilometres offshore — but I'm convinced that he'll do what he can to be home before she goes. Whatever their plans, it's not going to be easy on anyone.

One of the issues that isn't talked about enough is how difficult it is for families in outlying areas to send their kids to college or university. Not only is it more challenging emotionally — shipping your kids off four years before townies have to — it's crippling financially. Urban kids can go in search of post-secondary education and never have to leave their family home. Rural children, on the other hand, not only have to learn to live a new lifestyle, they need to find ways to help pay for it all. That's no small chore in a country where politicians download all the responsibility they can regarding the cost of educating our children. Government has decided that although they and big business benefit greatly from academic advancement — in the form of increased taxes and incredible employees — parents and their children have to subsidize this economic growth. Imagine what four years of student housing costs a rural family compared to urbanites who can send their kids off to school from the familiarity of their front porch. And picture shipping out an unseasoned seventeen-year-old outport person at the end of August, knowing that you won't see them again until Christmas.

One of my McCallum buddies loaned me a copy of *Maclean's* magazine dated March 1, 1982. That periodical was the first issue of Canada's weekly national news journal to be published after the sinking of the *Ocean Ranger*, Newfoundland's ill-fated oil rig. My buddy thought I might find these articles interesting, and I did — sort of. I love Canadian history, but very little causes me to feel as much grief as stories about other people's pain. Stories like the one about two thousand people piling into St. John's Roman Catholic basilica for a non-denominational service while thousands watched on television, praying that they could breathe out the sorrow that the sea brings to so many Newfoundland lives.

I was twenty-three years old at the time of that tragedy, and, not entirely in tune with current events, I wasn't paying a lot of attention to the Newfoundland news. Yet I know now that I was no different than the majority of men on the *Ocean Ranger*. I would have seen the opportunity to make $20,000 per year, at a time when magazines cost a dollar, as an incredible opportunity. Especially at an age when I saw myself as indestructible. So if my travels had taken me to the North Atlantic instead of the South Pacific, I could easily have accepted a job on the *Ocean Ranger*.

Initial reports suggested that the men onboard that rig included fifty-four Newfoundlanders, fourteen mainlanders, fourteen Americans, a Brit, and, when *Maclean's* went to press, one undisclosed nationality. Fathers, friends, brothers, sons, husbands, uncles . . . although it was obviously a time when, unlike today, women weren't hired to do that work, I think it's alright to imagine that crew could have included any of us in that era. It could have been you and me facing seventy-five-knot winds and seventy-eight-foot waves from a platform only seventy feet above sea level. It could have been any of us unsure of what was happening, what to do in response, or how to do it. Especially when she began to list fifteen degrees to the port side, at which point a distress signal was sent out.

Thirty minutes later, communication fell silent. An hour after that, three emergency vessels and two Sikorsky helicopters that had launched into gale winds arrived on the scene. Upon arrival, however, search and rescue saw nothing where the world's largest oil rig was supposed to be.

For a long time, that was all anyone could say about what had happened. All anybody knew for sure was that the *Ocean Ranger* had disappeared, sinking in 250 feet of water 324 kilometres east of St. John's, taking all on board with her. It was only onshore where things played out in a predictable way. After initially refusing to issue public statements, government and the oil business quickly went to work pointing fingers at each other while insurance companies looked for a place to hide. Newfoundlanders were forced to find their own ways to reconcile the loss of loved ones. Even those who knew no one on board get teary-eyed when they talk about it today.

eighteen

I've been living in McCallum for five years. It seems to me
that, in that time, the speed of life on the mainland has
increased. I see no indication that this nation's need for
speed won't continue, or that anyone can do anything about
it. As much as people beg for balance in their lives, governments and businesses are every day making decisions that
result in life getting harder and faster for everyone except
those with huge wealth.

Mainlanders are already moving as quickly as they can, to and from stores, schools, work, and all the appointments, play dates, and additional classes they've created for their kids. It's a wonder they're not all sick from a lack of real rest. Canada is copying Asian nations, so our politicians must be secretly planning on a population of at least a billion people — many of whom will work hard for almost nothing — because our current economic model is based on unlimited growth and low-cost labour. Mainlanders living in the lower ranks — the middle class no longer exists, just the filthy rich and the rest of us — don't seem to see this trend as a loss of life. Those with the least are losing time, money, and health, yet all they want to do is spend, buy, and borrow.

When I was a child in Ontario in the sixties, adults told me that one day I would only work four days per week. It's easy to see how such assumptions were made. That period in time saw huge attention paid to quality of life concerns. People had experienced years of sacrifice and no longer wished to do so. New technologies like fully automatic washing machines and oil-fired furnaces were increasingly providing folks with freedom from chores and responsibilities. Even governments of that era wanted to spend on services that improved people's lives — health services for example. And education.

So why did that train come off the tracks? I'm pretty sure that the answer has to do with how humans placed the economy on a higher level of importance than everything else on earth. More important than personal well-being, family, and the environment. I think this happened for two reasons. One: we all wanted more *stuff*, so we set out to make extra money in order to acquire these additional objects. Two: our desire to purchase these possessions played right into the hands of elected officials whose mandate is the making of money — governments' highest, adored, and often only priority. In other words, the more we work, and the more we spend, the more money we give to government. Politicians love this sheep-like quality about us, to a point where they prey upon it.

That's why politicians dislike rural Newfoundlanders so much. Because not only do rural Newfoundlanders refuse to choose Canada's economic hamster wheel ahead of a simple life they love, but they actually, on occasion, choose to access employment insurance paid into for the purpose of protecting themselves through tough times. Not only do a lot of rural Newfoundlanders *not* buy into the idea that making and spending money is life's most important priority, they occasionally take a little out of the public pot, to protect their right to live peacefully. It drives politicians crazy and renders townies and mainlanders resentful, that so many Newfoundlanders have found a way to not only live a balanced life, but to do so using what so many others see as *their* money.

I'm not really living like a rural Newfoundlander. I'm obviously trying, and I'm getting closer, but I'm not there yet. I don't qualify for any support, and I'm not at a point yet where I can consistently resist consuming. I am still caught in some kind of pathetic pattern where I buy things I shouldn't when I'm experiencing emotional pain. Then I find myself reading job postings — for work I don't want — when it's time to pay up.

Even in an isolated outport a person can sign onto eBay anytime they're feeling sad, low, or lonely — I think that's why so many outport women have been buying lapdogs of late. Purchasing anything has become quite easy. Plus, with satellite technology, outport people watch the same television — the same influential ads — as everyone else. I'm convinced that's how I got suckered into buying a new car recently while visiting friends and family in Ontario. I live in an isolated Newfoundland community that contains *no* cars. Most days, I embrace that way of living — I want my lifelong love affair with the internal combustion engine to officially be over — but the minute I'm around automobiles again, the car-loving little boy in me kicks in and I go shopping.

At least this time I bought an economy car, I tell myself — an economy car with a twist. It's a rally car. I'd tell you the manufacturer's name, but I don't want to advertise for the world's wealthiest. It's got a six-speed gearbox, and I had an exhaust specialist put an aftermarket muffler on it to give it a more masculine sound, if you can call a two-litre motor manly.

When you consider how infrequently I drive — once every three months or more — I shouldn't own a vehicle at all. It makes no sense. But when the opportunity presents itself, I do enjoy the open road, including my three-thousand-kilometre trek from Kitchener to McCallum. Once past Montreal's dangerous drivers and inadequate infrastructure, driving alongside the St. Lawrence River is a good way to do some serious thinking. And while New Brunswick's unsustainable logging practices are hard to miss, and stomach, there are still some things worth pondering about that province. Like how magical that wilderness must have been before the chainsaw was invented.

Then it's on to Nova Scotia, including Cape Breton, where not only the vistas are different, the people are too.

They're more distinctive, individually, in a subtle sort of way. After a lengthy wait in a no-longer-proud-and-productive North Sydney on a tarmac filled with idling transport trucks, I catch an overnight ferry across the Cabot Strait. Taking an overnighter saves having to spend a day in the company of a boatful of Marine Atlantic employees who give the impression that smiling is against Crown policies. It's unbelievable how some of the friendliest people in the world — Atlantic Canadians — suddenly turn sour after they obtain employment with a federally owned agency.

The next morning, I race out of my cabin excited for an opportunity to catch a glimpse of Newfoundland's Southwest Coast shrouded in fog. I love that look and never tire of it. It represents adventure to me. I find it exhilarating to know that that landscape doesn't look a whole lot different today than it did when Captain Cook first saw it. But it's not until I escape the run-down town of Port aux Basques — our re-entry point — that I feel like I've arrived. My feet don't feel firmly back on Newfoundland rock until I'm travelling among mountains. So if there aren't any 140-kilometre winds to worry about while passing through the appropriately named Wreckhouse region — where I've seen a fully loaded transport truck blow over — I'll spend the next couple hours watching the sun come up over the Codroy Valley.

Knowing that no matter what time I arrive in Newfoundland, incompatible ferry schedules will not permit me to reach McCallum until the following day, I try to make this next leg of my journey joyful. I go out of my way to find curvy coastal roads, and I explore communities that I can only access by automobile. I want to experience them all. Yet, whatever route I travel, I always end that first day of Newfoundland driving at Grand Falls-Windsor — a former pulp and paper town with all the unattractive shortcomings that come with such a big-business beginning. I make Grand Falls-Windsor my last stop of the day because GFW is my last chance to purchase the consumer products that my neighbours and I will want and need upon my return to McCallum. It's not uncommon to haul a greasy bucket of Kentucky Fried Chicken for five hours for someone in need of a fix. That chicken's stench is one of the reasons I made sure my new car had a separate trunk and not a hatchback.

An early start the next morning ensures that I can get to Hermitage in time to wash my car clean with creek water and slip it into the space that the Sandyville Inn provides me for free. As my thirty-hour drive comes to a close, I comfort myself with the thought that I'm now only a ninety-minute boat ride from home.

I'm sure it's confusing for listeners when they hear me

talk of "home." I tell Newfoundlanders I'm going home when I intend to travel to Ontario, and I tell mainlanders I'm heading home when returning to Newfoundland. Do people who move away always have two homes and the heartache that comes with such a situation? If not, how long do you have to live in one locale before such sadness ceases? Not just that your choice of location becomes the house where you most frequently hang your hat, but the place where you feel, in your heart, is where you need to spend a lot of time if you hope to stay healthy and happy. I've never had that contented feeling. I've always felt conflicted.

I lived in Australia for more than a year but it never felt like home to me. As great as those Aussies are, I never thought of staying. Even the warm weather wasn't appealing enough to make me want to live there long term. Yet it was Australia where the pull of the open ocean first made its mark on me, and where I began to enjoy different dialects.

I also spent nine months in Alberta, driving a snowcat for a ski resort 7,200 feet above sea level. Although the work I did, and skiing from October to June, was a joy, nothing else about Alberta made me want to stay there. So I went to Ontario cottage country, where I bought a little beach house that I later traded in for a large farm in Fenelon Falls. But even those gorgeous pieces of property just became annoying mortgages after a while, obstacles that interfered with me quitting one more good job and moving on.

I am afflicted with a feeling that wherever I am, I think I'm supposed to be somewhere else. It's not that I don't try to get excited at the prospect of settling down, minding my own business, making good . . . it's just that that only increases my urge to move on. As much as I enjoyed what all those great places had to offer, I didn't feel my heart tugging me towards permanent residence in any of them. So I shouldn't be surprised when I can't convince Newfoundlanders that I'm here to stay. I told a friend who lives in Gaultois that I don't think the people in his community like me. He said, "It's not that they don't like you — it's that they don't under-stand why you're here."

The Southwest Coast isn't the only region that finds fellers from away confusing. Many Newfoundlanders don't trust mainlanders. I understand how this happened. Decades of neglect, mismanagement, and bad treatment by those counted on to lead can turn anyone bitter. So it doesn't surprise me when Newfoundlanders direct their day-to-day distrust at Ontario. What I do find strange is the way so many urban Newfoundlanders are copying the mainland's most unattractive attributes — the way Newfoundlanders are acting more and more like mainlanders. The way they flip houses, for example, after years of nurturing their home for the purpose of providing for their people. Urban Newfoundlanders today see their houses as simply something to sell. What not that long ago was a labour of love is now about making money.

And what about the distance that Newfoundland residents now travel to and from employment? There are companies flying Newfoundlanders back and forth to Alberta for six days of work wedged between four-day weekends — half of which the worker spends travelling to and fro. This kind of commute makes ninety-minute stop-and-go drives on Ontario's 400-series highways look like a leisurely stroll.

I once took an early morning flight from Deer Lake to Toronto that was scheduled to continue on to Calgary. All of us onboard were Newfoundland residents, but I was the only passenger who didn't know everyone else. I was also the only one excited about the trip. Window blinds were quickly closed so everyone could catch up on their shortage of shut-eye. A man wearing a camouflaged cap recognized a guy in a t-shirt celebrating the Newfoundland town of Dildo. "How's it goin'?" he asked, before his buddy threw him a sarcastic comeback: "Oh, you know — livin' the dream." And what about the personal debt that so many of today's Newfoundlanders so willingly take on? Big trucks, fancy cabins, ATVs, snowmobiles, monster houses, leases, loans, mortgages . . . even the accumulation of toys is so *not* Newfoundland — the urge to stuff your garage with gear when, once upon a time, filling your shed with friends was seen as so much more satisfying.

Ironically, there's change afoot elsewhere in Canada where urbanites are trying to copy Newfoundlanders of years gone by — choosing to see their homes as something other than an investment. Folks who are trying to carry less debt, buy fewer toys, keep free-range chickens, and be nicer to each other. Voters who are aligning themselves with leaders who care about the less fortunate. In places where commuters are trying to travel shorter distances, by bicycle, to and from satisfying work, while Newfoundlanders learn to live like suburban Torontonians.

Part Three

nineteen

It was one of the few things that got more funding in last
year's budget, amid a sea of cuts, but since the government
bumped up the incentive for resettlement, there haven't been
any new takers. "I would hope that more communities would
explore this in the future, but there's certainly no pressure
from government for them to do so," said Municipal Affairs
Minister Steve Kent, who's responsible for resettlement issues.

— James McLeod, *The St. John's Telegram*, May 24, 2014

When Steve Kent says, "There's certainly no pressure from government for [outport people to consider resettling elsewhere]," he is either lying or seriously lacking in smarts. No wonder my McCallum neighbours constantly question how often the former Mount Pearl mayor gets off the Avalon Peninsula, Newfoundland's only real urban region. Perhaps Kent meant that government is applying no *direct* pressure, because it's obvious around here that politicians are applying as much indirect pressure as they possibly can without alienating voters who are sympathetic to the out-port person's predicament. And that's just a gutless way of going about your business. If government wants people out of the outports, they should shut those communities down instead of insisting on making it look like they had no role in the outcome.

Take a look at Little Bay Islands, another isolated out-port in a situation similar to McCallum. Little Bay Islands' resettlement vote is stuck at 89.47 percent in favour of going (.53 percent under the arbitrarily assigned requirement). I've been to Little Bay Islands. It's a lovely little community, but it feels like a funeral home. I would walk around town every day and never see a soul. There is only one learner left in the Little Bay Islands school. Yet the municipal affairs minister has adamantly stated that Little Bay Islands does not qualify for resettlement money, leaving residents to further sort out their sad situation on their own.

Does anybody really believe that dangling a quarter of a million dollars, and insisting on ninety percent community approval before anyone can collect doesn't create consider-able "pressure" for the people the incentive program is aimed at? For the ones who can't read or write — to find them-selves in a position where they have to consider leaving their isolated ancestral home, talking to strangers (even signing on the dotted line with one of them should they wish to purchase a new house) — any hint at all that they're going to have to go is incredibly difficult for them to deal with. And just because there are outsiders who don't understand the relationship these outport people have with the land they grew up on doesn't mean such an earthly connection doesn't exist or isn't important. Anyone who thinks these people haven't experienced extreme pressure since March 26, 2013 — the day this generation's resettlement offer was tendered — is hugely mistaken.

This is not urban Ontario. Speculators are not buying up homes in isolated outports in hope of one day acquiring some easy resettlement money. It just doesn't work that way. Before you can collect, you have to have lived in your home for six months plus a day, per year, for the two years prior to accepting the province's offer. And should that day come, when ninety percent of your people vote to go, the province has stated it would be at least two or three years after that before someone would receive any money. And we all know how government works — "two or three years" usually turns out to be a whole lot longer. So the value of homes around here has actually plummeted since the resettlement proposal was put forward. Outport people are now hard-pressed to get $500 for a home that, prior to the province's resettlement offer, might have fetched them five thousand.

Government is not offering to purchase our homes — they're trying to buy us out. It's simple math. They no longer want to service us. If paying everyone resettlement money costs less than the price of servicing a town for twenty years, that community qualifies to collect. This ratio rationale is easy to achieve when you weigh in the replacement cost of a ferry. So grief is everywhere, as is all its associated anger, bargaining, and depression.

McCallum is not an easy place to be these days. After two years of trying to convince the crowd who wants to stay to see their way, the gang who wants to go is threatening to leave anyway — without the money. Some will go forever, others only for the winter. Some people are already managing their absences this way for lifestyle-related reasons, others out of anger. They're sending a message to those who want to stay. They're saying, "You want to stay? Okay. Then here is what it's going to look like: There won't be forty-five people here. So the ferry won't come [as often]. And there won't be anybody to play darts with, or shovel your snow, or fix your pipes when they freeze. No sir, you'll have to feel lonely like I do."

I can tell you that's difficult. As capable and hardy as these outport people are, they do not want to be by themselves. When you travel rural Ontario, you see single homes sitting all alone almost everywhere, whereas in Newfoundland, you can drive miles without seeing any sign of civilization, but when you do come across development, you discover a cluster of homes, all of which sit surprisingly close to one another. That's because a lot of Newfoundlanders like to live in rural environments, but in no way do they wish to be there alone. They even build their weekend wilderness cabins close to one another because they don't want to be too far from the people they care about.

Me? I like my own company and can withstand being alone for longer than most, but, by saying that, I don't intend to underestimate the importance of community. If you insisted I live a couple kilometres outside of McCallum's infrastructure, I would die. Not only because the absence of physical support and protection would quickly cost me my life — I need others around me as well.

I've been eating supper at Lloyd and Linda Durnford's home every Sunday for five years. They're my best friends east of Ontario. I drop in after men's darts, and one or two other nights per week. Maybe more. Clyde and Flora Feaver feed me almost as often, and several other families fill in around that committed crew. When I travel the eastern part of this province, I use Glen Cook and Daphne Fudge's St. John's home as my base. I love their young girl and their old dog, and I really do enjoy St. John's. Daphne is a former McCallum resident, and Glen's a great guy from Markland, one of Newfoundland's rare inland communities that started as an experimental agriculture project.

But even with all these wonderful people in my Newfoundland life, I still ache for my Ontario friends and family. When my young nieces in Waterloo attend karate class, I wish I was there to watch. Or if my Ontario buddies go to a movie, it hurts that I can't tag along. One of the loneliest nights of my life occurred when my youngest sister — a musician — accompanied Northern Pikes frontman Jay Semko in a Kitchener concert that I couldn't attend because I was in McCallum.

Mostly, however, I wish I had a significant other to share all this with. It's possible I'd be content anywhere in Canada if I had someone special by my side who wanted to be there with me. I can go it alone if I have to, but I don't want to. Never is this more obvious than when I hike Newfoundland high country, because I believe beautiful scenery is better when it's shared. I'm hardwired to love the long view, and, oh my god, Newfoundland has some luscious scenery I want to continue to indulge in. Just not alone.

I'm going to Grips Nest, a respected McCallum climb that is most challenging after a heavy snowfall like the one we just had. I tell Lloyd and Linda, "If I'm not back for supper at Matt and Sarah's, you know where to start looking for me." I am travelling light, and alone. I am sporting good footwear but no snowshoes or crampons to keep me from falling through or slipping back.

It's not long before I realize that I don't know where I am. Not that I haven't hiked Grips Nest by myself before, but I haven't gone in the snow. I can see that, in the past, I've simply followed a well-worn trail, walking in the footsteps of those who came before me. Today I have to decide for myself the best path to the summit. This trip, my self-confidence and decision-making talents will be tested as much as my climbing judgement and physical fitness. I'll have to create my own stairway to heaven, driving the toe of my boot into terrain in such a way that allows me to inch my way up — a process easier said than done when, every three or four steps, my boot breaks through the crust cover into a leg-swallowing snowdrift. I learn to avoid areas where stunted fir trees grow, because they serve to collect considerable snow. Fortunately, for parts of this climb, there is the occasional alder to hang onto when I need to catch my breath or pull myself to safety.

As I reach higher heights, the reflected sun on my face becomes a primary source of pleasure. As does the increasingly expanding view. Even seeing twenty sickly salmon cages can't discourage my day when I reach the top and look out at the spectacular 360-degree views such elevation provides — several pretty peninsulas, an enormous assortment of high hills, the France-owned islands of St. Pierre et Miquelon, and my little house a long way away. It's moments exactly like these that I wish I had a woman with me. A view like this is 250,000 times better when you share it. Especially if you bring along a big blanket, because it's a gift to be able to make love someplace like Grips Nest, where nobody can hear the rapture — a serious consideration when you live in an outport where no one is more than a kilometre from everyone else and sound carries across water the way it does.

But right now, there is no room for sorrowful feelings or sexy thoughts. Today, the top of Grips Nest is icy, making travel tricky. So after paying a brief tribute to the profound spirits that can be found at lofty levels — Grips Nest is as good a place as any to say hello to my deceased sister — I start down, a journey that at first consideration should be easier than my upward climb, but instead requires some serious attention. A slight slip can easily result in a rocky ride, an abrupt stop, or dramatic drop. Or, worse yet, maybe even a missed supper at Matt and Sarah's.

Matt and Sarah have also suffered. The loss of their son Reguel, who died in his sleep of diabetes-related illnesses at the age of forty-three, was a catastrophe for the Fudge family. I never knew Reguel, but around here, I hear his name all the time. So whenever I visit his sister Daphne's family in St. John's, I ask for more detail regarding Reguel's life.

A diligent worker, Daphne's efforts to communicate are no less conscientious. "Michael, Sandra, and Reguel were all delivered by midwife in McCallum," she'll tell me. "But the rest — Alvin, Tracy, my twin brother, Danny, and I — were born in the Harbour Breton hospital. Reguel was the second oldest.

"While Reguel had to go to Port aux Basques for one year of high school, it's fair to say McCallum had always been his home, and that he'd never really left. Because immediately after finishing school, Reguel came home to fish. He loved everything about the outdoors — fishing, hunting, trouting, going to the cabin for two or three nights with the boys . . . Reguel had lots he liked to do. But he did it all very quietly. He loved to read. And he minded his own business in a genuinely friendly way.

"I remember one of the first times I took Glen to McCallum. We were allowed to catch our fifteen fish [quota]. I went out on the boat with my dad, and Reguel and Glen went out in Reguel's boat. I guess I'm competitive, but Dad and I were trying to get our fish before Glen and Reguel did. So I fought off some seasickness while Dad and I went as fast as we could. Yet there was Reguel and Glen waiting for us when we got back. And not only did they catch their fifteen fish faster than we did, their fish were bigger than ours."

The same age now as her brother was when he died, Daphne is well aware of the pain that Reguel's death inflicted on her family. "My best memories of Reguel are from when I was a small child. Because, eight years younger than he was, I became quite attached to him. When I look back at old pictures, I was always in his arms. I remember one day, when I was six, Reguel was taking me, Tracy, and Danny to school. This was before McCallum had boardwalks, and I fell down right in front of Hartland and Lillian's house. I was more scared than hurt, but Reguel still took the time to take me home. After I stopped crying, he walked me back.

"He was a gentle guy who would faint at the sight of blood if he cut himself. Obviously, he overcame that sensitivity when he had to start sticking needles in himself [for his diabetes]. And it felt like he overcame it for me, too. Because I remember a time when I scalded my arm, and another day when I cut my head open. When things like that would happen, I would sleep beside him so he could keep an eye on me. And it's this way we became attached to each other that I like to remember him. I like to remember Reguel as my big brother." A sibling connection I can easily comprehend.

twenty

*"We knows we have to go," said one woman, who admitted
she had never lived anywhere else.*
 I asked how old she was.
 "Eighty-two this year."
 "Where will you go?"
 She laughed. "I haven't got a clue."

— Michael Crummey, Special to the *Globe and Mail*,
 August 15, 2014

In his little book *Journeys of Simplicity*, Philip Harnden pays
attention to the travel plans of the Arctic tern, an annual
visitor to my McCallum home and, because of its elegant
form and erratic flight pattern, my favourite seabird:

*During summer these birds nest in Greenland, Alaska,
Canada, and islands of the Arctic. In autumn some migrate
south along the Pacific coast of the Americas. Others fly east
over the Atlantic, then south past Europe and Africa to the*

*Antarctic Circle. In the spring they retrace their route, for
an annual round trip of more than 22,000 miles.*

*In 1970 an Arctic tern trapped alive in Maine had a leg
band showing it to be thirty-four years old. In its lifetime
it had probably flown some 750,000 miles, much of that
over open seas. It weighed 4½ ounces. It was rebanded and
released.*

Harnden closes his account of this intriguing enigma by noting that, for the tern's entire thirty-five-thousand-kilometre migration, it brings along no baggage, a feature I find inspiring. Because if the day ever arrives where I need to depart my McCallum home permanently, I plan on leaving with as little as I can. I'll bring one or two bags containing clothing that can help me withstand the weather, and a nice shirt and jeans that will allow me to feel comfortable in most social environments.

None of the other attachments I've carried around this world will be welcome on the voyage. None of the hundreds of books I'll no longer read, the building materials I accumulated in the event I *might* need them, or the coffee mugs no one ever drinks from. I'm mostly through with personal possessions. I'm going to sell my car and plan to never own another. I want to find a way to walk. I've discovered a lot about nature in this outport because I'm not enclosed in an automobile as I come and go. I've learned how to hear a porpoise in the harbour long before I see it. I recognize the blast from its blowhole before I even lift my head to look. After years of living in urban areas, or on a large piece of property previously ruled by the plough, I never would have guessed that, in coastal Newfoundland, on a simple spring stroll, one can see an enormous number of migrating warblers.

Even if I settle in another city, I can't imagine needing more than a tiny apartment containing a comfortable bed and a table that can double as a desk. I've discovered that home ownership can cost you the freedom to turn down work that only sustains you in economic ways. I'll no longer have any part of that. I will never again take on a load, financial or otherwise, without careful consideration.

My intent to refuse to continuously consume feels right in other ways as well. I'm sick of buying things that I thought would bring me some kind of sustainable happiness. They didn't, and never will. Plus, as long as I insist on following the artist's path, I'll probably always have cash-flow concerns. So I need to find other ways to acquire joy.

I jump out of bed in anticipation of a day of writing, or hiking. Even when we go lobster fishing or in search of moose in the wee hours of the morning, I don't need an alarm. Not that I haven't occasionally set one, but I've never needed it. I'm always too excited to sleep and have consistently been up when my wake-up call came. Living with this kind of anticipation can be exhausting, but I wouldn't trade it for the world.

How does a person arrive at a point where they'll choose potential poverty over what Edward Abbey called "syphilization"? For me, it has come with realizing that much of what I know is not true, and that if I have any hope of recovering from the socioeconomic lies I've been told since childhood, I need to look at what my heart is trying to tell me, and why.

My life has been driven by a huge, hungry, angry ego that insisted on being kept safe. I bagged adventures and experiences like they were trophies, and I insatiably sought attention. I chased employment that facilitated my need to feed my self-image. I naively believed that formal education and a professional position meant I was smart and successful, and that any recognition I received supported such thoughts. "Follow me," I said in so many ways, "I've got it all figured out." But that was bullshit. So as I continue to recalibrate my midcourse correction, I wonder what it all needs to look like.

Perhaps I could fill my days demonstrating day-to-day compassion. I want to love, and be loved. The more I give, the more I get. I don't just mean as it applies to others — it is time I am kinder to myself. I only want to do work that permits me to steer clear of *the man*. People only motivated by power and/or money are miserable. I don't just mean the people who rule the private sector — some of the most ruthless, power-hungry men and women I know run our public institutions. I want as much distance between me and those egomaniacs as I can manage. I want control over my workday.

I'm pleased that my publisher is indie, and that I don't have an agent. I'm following the recording artists who don't sell out to the thieves at Ticketmaster. But that's only about my business plan, and that hardly seems important anymore. It's my friends and family that matter most.

Janet's mom, Joyce, once told me a person can go around the world a million times in his or her heart. She wanted me to understand how rich a life can be, even when experienced in the narrowest of physical confines. And, while I trusted her enough to remember such wisdom, it has taken me twenty years to see a pathway to Joyce's profoundness. So, while world travel is enlightening, it's not hockey card collecting — I no longer need to keep a checklist.

I don't need a bucket list either. I've done what I had to. If I should die today, feel whatever you need to for yourself, but don't shed a tear for me. I plan to live a whole lot longer, but if I don't, know that I was okay with that. I don't want to fear aging, illness, and death. Resistance is pointless.

After a lifetime of trying to be a big-shot, I'm going to get *smaller*. I'm going to return to Ontario, that ugly old ogre I've been running from. I need to face the demons I left behind, reacquaint myself with family and friends, and find new ways to make my manifesto work. Plus, I need more children around. One of the greatest challenges of living in McCallum is that there are too few children. I've never liked the feel of an adults-only community, and with a grownup-to-child ratio of thirteen to one, McCallum's kids don't need me. I'd like to find a child or two that wishes for adult attention. Maybe I can coach some Little League baseball.

With any luck at all I'll fall in love again, and hopefully that relationship will go the distance this time. It has often crossed my mind that I might be able to assist someone in an unfortunate situation — someone who wants and needs what I have to give. I may finally be at a point in my own maturity where I can support another in her efforts to heal, without me taking all her pain personally. My McCallum neighbours have taught me this. It's amazing how well they find ways to work with each other — to the point of making peace with some highly damaged individuals.

The close confines of an isolated outport never permit you to completely get away from those you don't want to be around. Including your enemies. Whether you're playing for the same darts team or part of a group effort to re-shingle someone's roof, McCallum requires constant courteousness and compassion. It's so unlike the city that way. If the sun is setting over the Gulf of St. Lawrence, and you notice the neighbour who stole a can of gas from your shed last summer hasn't come home from his cabin, you don't allow your anger to stop you from preparing a search party at the possibility that this shady character might be clinging to a cold, slippery rock in the North Atlantic. Because without each other, we're all dead in the water.

Yet, as much as I love to assist my elders, the load that comes with doing so in McCallum has become increasingly large. One early morning, I helped stretcher a badly suffering senior to the ferry. Four of us had to cart that man and gurney down a steep, slippery, snakelike stairway. Two of my earnest coworkers were in their seventies, and the other was fighting cancer. I was glad to help — even honoured to be asked — but I remember thinking that I, at fifty-something, with a bad back, should not be the youngest, healthiest man here.

Many men figured this out before I did — that the

number of McCallum males up for assisting the elderly with their chores has been exceeded by the number in need — and that this imbalance is unbearable some days, like when a storm is approaching and everyone's boat needs to be pulled from the water. The able men have made themselves scarce. "I want to help, but my own work isn't getting done," I've heard several guys say. This burden alone has caused some amazing men to move away. Aging is hard on everyone.

Never are the pressures on outport people greater than they are at Christmas. Whether you're one of those who stays or goes — almost nobody comes — it's a tough time of year. For those who stay, they run the risk of being house-bound and all alone. I don't imagine a solitary life is a good substitute for the Christmases these people remember from their past, when crazy youngsters, kitchen parties, mummers, and ice skating on Brandy Pond were a twelve-day way of life. And for those who leave town in search of loved ones, travel can be difficult when bad weather puts their trip, and lives, at risk. Newfoundland roads are not safe, and death doesn't care whether it's Christmas.

Those who work on trawlers, or in the oil fields, also feel considerable sadness over the holidays when their bosses don't recognize the ways in which low morale actually hinders a worker's capacity to make money for those who employ them.

Then there's the group who unselfishly take time away from their families in order to maintain essential services for the rest of us. Our nurses, for example, and those who keep our ferries afloat. These aren't easy absences either.

As for the gang that spends the holidays hanging around the outport, they do what they can to make the most of the season — decorating their homes, sharing delicious meals — but time can be long when you're miles from your children and your grandchildren except for the occasional heart-wrenching phone call on Christmas day. Even webcam technology — the chance to witness a grandchild opening a gift in Grande Prairie, perhaps — is less and less an option, what with governments increasingly dumping an inadequate internet infrastructure on rural Newfoundlanders in hope that every inconvenience they can impose on people will eventually force them to move to the city.

I've spent a few Christmases away — first in Melbourne, then Banff, and now in McCallum — and, despite the surfing, skiing, and tasty dinners I indulged in, each absence brought me sizeable suffering. I understand what outport people feel when they are far away from those who they care most deeply for. In fact, Christmas can be hard even when you're *surrounded* by loved ones. Just ask fifty-seven-year-old Ralph Coles of Bonavista Bay.

"No, my buddy, this is going to be a Christmas like none before," the St. John's taxi driver strongly states. He is taking me to the airport so I can spend my first Christmas with family in a long time. Unclear of what Ralph is trying to tell me, I ask for clarification. "Well, my son," he says, "last week the doctor told my wife she has breast cancer. And, while I know a lot of people is scared off by the 'C' word — there seems to be a lot more cancer around than there were when we was kids — me and my girls are not afraid. I mean all eight of 'em. We've got seven daughters, the wife and I do, and they are all grown up and educated except the youngest, and she will be going to university in Halifax next year. The others are in Yellowknife, Gander, Brampton, Dubai, and we got two in Calgary.

"I always said I would do what I could to make money — I built boats before the fishery crashed — but that every penny we saved had to be put to helping our girls get schooled. I am not one of those men who thinks women should not go to school."

A likeable little guy, Ralph is a distracted driver. Following the car in front of us far too close for my comfort, he has to apply his brakes more often than I think necessary. I do understand, however, why he might have other matters on his mind. "Her cancer is treatable," he tells me. "That's what the doctor says. The doctor is a woman too. She is going to take the lump out, in January, and she wants to get a look at the other lymph nodes while she is in there. If those nodes are cancer free, and me and my girls are saying they will be, then my wife can get radiation, and we know that can beat a person down, don't we?" But before I can reply, Ralph has another question: "Did I say that right — lymph nodes?" I assure him that the words he uses, and the way he says them, are correct, but even if they weren't, Ralph Coles has made himself clearly understood — he is expecting this coming Christmas to be like none he and his courageous crew have ever experienced.

twenty-one

Linda Hennessey, the chair of McCallum's relocation committee, refers to McCallum as "a dying community. The population of the community drops to between 40–50 people during the winter months, with the others coming back to spend their summers. The school has only six students this year and, with one graduating high school in June, there will only be five students going back in September." She worries that these children and youth are missing out on important socialization skills.

— Danette Dooley, *Grand Falls-Windsor Advertiser*, June 2, 2015

I don't mean Linda Hennessey any harm — she's worked hard at a tough job that no one else wanted, including me — but I don't believe she should comment publicly on whether McCallum's "children and youth are missing out on important socialization skills." I don't think anyone should. To discuss among your family and friends about how staying in a dying outport might affect the development of a child's socialization skills is fair territory. But to tell newspaper reporters, and go on social media, open-line radio, and television news, to speak about your concerns regarding other parents' choices to keep their children in an arguable situation? That's not right. That might be the meanest way in which resettlement is presently playing out — people all over this province are publicly suggesting that raising your children in an isolated outport stunts their growth.

I can see how the aggressors got to this insensitive place — if you're desperate to move someone along, and they resist your efforts, you might be frustrated enough to indirectly toss the occasional hurtful comment in your opposition's direction. And there's no more surefire way to do that than to tell them that they're hurting their children. But such a choice is uncharitable, and self-degrading if you stand to make money from it.

I often get asked if I believe McCallum's children suffer socially, given they are such a small group. I don't think so, I say. I'm seeing so many of them do so incredibly well for themselves after they leave the outport that for me to suggest otherwise would be misguided on my part. I also point out that afflictions like social anxiety are not exclusive to outport people — lots of big-city residents are shy around strangers and overwhelmed upon entering a big arena. Then I tell those doing the asking that it's outport people who have previously moved away that I'm most uneasy about, because there are some really inconsiderate thinkers in that group who have way too much to say about this sensitive subject. I wonder how these commentators can, in good conscience, constantly suggest that because *they* attended a school that had a whopping fifty-four learners, they're somehow socially superior. This self-centred way of seeing the world frustrates me so much I've occasionally found it necessary to confront these critics.

I wish more people could acknowledge the amazing upside that results when you have one teacher for every three or four students, as you do in McCallum. I've seen firsthand how fruitful this situation can be for those kinds of learners who would surely receive less attention in a more populated environment. There were seventeen hundred students at my high school, a number that did not work in my favour. Yet I can guarantee you that no child slips through the cracks in McCallum these days, because McCallum loves its children.

Not that everyone everywhere doesn't care about their kids, just that events like Halloween remind me how much the people of McCallum look out for the children in their community. McCallum's pumpkin-heads collect much larger piles of loot than you'd expect from a town with only twenty-five homes to hand out candy. If the children in McCallum imagine that kids in the city get more, they're wrong.

McCallum knows exactly how many children will be trick-or-treating. So families don't have to budget what they buy at the store or give out at the door, unlike city people who never know from year to year how many kids could be arriving and are cautious with their handouts as a result. So while it may look like children in the city have an unlimited number of houses to collect candy from, a night's take for a townie is no greater than it is for a bay-kid in McCallum, and the tricksters don't have to cover as many miles to amass it.

With so few goblins participating in this ritual pillage of the village, and with everyone knowing these children so well, McCallum folks are extremely generous, some even picking up fancy chocolate in the city so as to provide diversity among the mix. Plus, McCallum candy costs considerably less than Halloween sweets in the city, because, while Fudge's Store intends to turn a profit, city stores look to make a killing. In the city, large faceless chain stores don't hesitate to swindle customers on special occasions, unlike a little family-owned outfit in an outport, which simply prices everything with its usual markup. So a big box of little potato-chip bags in McCallum costs half as much as it does in the city, and the children benefit from that difference when the locals spend their savings on additional treats.

My favourite part of an outport Halloween is knowing

that the night this event occurs can be decided at supper-time on the thirty-first of October. If heavy rain or a community-wide flu bug comes to town, a couple of phone calls after supper can truly postpone the entire community's Halloween operations. Halloween doesn't happen until conditions are safe and ideal. McCallum's moms make sure of that. And the public criticism of McCallum's youngest and most vulnerable doesn't occur as often as it might either — not as long as I've got those kids covered.

So make no mistake about it, McCallum's relocation committee is *pro* resettlement — it's not a neutral board — and this is disappointing. This absence of balance makes the group that wants to stick around feel outnumbered more than ever, and it didn't have to happen that way. An equitable discussion among everyone could have been facilitated from the beginning. Government could easily have led such a conversation, and it would have cost them almost nothing. Instead they dumped this hot potato in the hands of some frustrated people who feel they have to oversimplify the situation in their efforts to move things along.

When you consider all the amazing skills that outport

people possess, working through a polarizing situation in a harmonious way is not one of them. I remember chairing a public meeting in McCallum regarding ferry issues. Doing so was as challenging a professional assignment as I've ever accepted. The community group that wanted change had some worthy concerns, but their conveyance of them was fuelled by relentless anger. I never saw the facilitation of a peaceful resolution as an option that I was allowed to choose as chair. I was expected to carry the torch for the angry group, and nothing else was seen as acceptable. Even a visiting teacher from another part of the province told me that my idea of presenting the committee's concerns in a balanced way was "one of the silliest things" she'd ever heard. "This is war," she firmly informed me, and no one disagreed. In the end, ferry personnel felt dumped on after receiving the news, via their employer, that McCallum was unhappy with their efforts, and I don't believe our run-in had to happen that way. I think we could have initiated change without anyone further feeling hurt.

So now, because the group that wishes to take the province's resettlement offer has done such a thorough job of alienating those who don't want to go, the crew that wants to stay has stubbornly dug in deeper than ever. So deep that even if this team that doesn't want to go was presented with an argument that might give them reason to reconsider, they wouldn't listen. As a consequence, there are no winners around here right now. And I find that unfortunate.

As for the outlying islanders who are watching the final days of this outport unfold from afar, and chiming in negative comments whenever it makes them feel good about themselves to do so, the idea that they're next — that once they've chased these outport people from their ancestral homes, the forces at work to destroy those who are different will turn their attention on *them* — is lost on these dissidents. This club of critics doesn't realize that the argument that these smaller communities are economically inefficient will eventually come around to bite them in the butt because, shortly after the final outport gasps its last breath, someone somewhere will point out that at first the smaller cities, and eventually the entire island, should be resettled on the grounds that they are an economic anchor tied to the rest of the province/ country. And once again, the aggressors will forget that there are real people affected by their rhetoric.

Yet, new ferries and the cost of running and maintaining them are indeed expensive. So much so that politicians have decided some special-interest groups — Fogo Island, for example, Newfoundland's equivalent to Disneyland — should get themselves a big, beautiful boat, while the rest of the communities are culled. So when the alternative is to be turned into a counterfeit tourist attraction like Quidi Vidi Village is, I think that outport people elsewhere should consider themselves lucky that their plug is being pulled. I'd rather see McCallum die a dignified death than become an amusement park for mainlanders. But that was never going to happen anyway — government has already secretly decided that the Southwest Coast is to be Newfoundland's newest industrial basin.

Few rural Newfoundlanders know what an industrial basin is. It's a townie term, I tell them. It's the place where city planners traditionally put their most unsightly, smelly, and environmentally unsound things. Factories, sewage treatment plants, auto wreckers, warehouses — it's where a community's appearance, health, and recreation opportunities are set aside in the name of making money.

Provincial governments create industrial basins as well, but on a much larger scale. The Newfoundland town of Buchans is a good example. If Canadian vacationers ever saw the former mining town in commercials and other ads, they'd spend their travel dollars in Detroit. Buchans looks like something out of a science-fiction movie where the earth's environment has been destroyed, and the poor souls who survived that disaster are desperately fighting over what few natural resources remain.

Now compare that apocalyptic vision to the outports of Burgeo, Ramea, Francois, Grey River, and Grand Bruit. The people in those drop-dead-gorgeous towns had a dream — a dream they were working on for ten years. The residents of those five communities wanted to create a National Marine Conservation Area around the cliffs and fiords of the Southwest Coast. So for a decade they worked together in an effort to utilize money that Prime Minister Jean Chrétien had set aside for just such ideas. For ten years, these towns worked not only with each other but with fishing and mining organizations to take control of their own destiny, rather than wait for their fishery to continue to collapse and for politicians to indirectly force them into accepting resettlement. But that was before the province of Newfoundland shut down their whole idea, saying government wasn't interested in any community conservation projects that might interfere with big business's efforts to further set up salmon cages and access minerals along the Southwest Coast. And, as if it wasn't painful enough that politicians denied these outport people of their dream, government kept that February 2012 decision a secret for an entire year, while those outport people laboured away. It was only when Parks Canada said they would like to go ahead with a study to see if such a park proposal was possible that the people working away learned that their politicians had already subversively sabotaged their efforts.

But at least now we know. If there is any silver lining in this snub, it's that Newfoundland's government has finally been forced to come clean. It's gotten clearer why government treats us the way they do, why they don't fix any road that might bring visitors down here, or set up a ferry schedule that would actually encourage tourists to travel this incredible coastline. It's because government wants this area for themselves. It's because they see this region as having as many ecologically insane salmon cages as they can stuff in every cove, bay, and fiord. It's because they want more mountains of mine tailings, and fewer mountain climbers. It's because they want oil rigs as far as the eye can see, like you'll find in the Gulf of Mexico from Alabama to Texas. It's because Newfoundland's leadership sees the Southwest Coast as some sort of garbage dump where they can hide their most unsightly, smelly, and environmentally unsound things.

twenty-two

Residents of McCallum voted on resettlement last week, but not enough people were in favour for the town to be eligible for government financial assistance . . . "While the government are saying that they have to think about everybody in the community, it's really difficult to believe that when we have more than 50 per cent of people that want to go," said Hennessey. "These people not only want to go, but they need to go." . . . "All the government has done is put a generous offer on the table, and they've created a lot of broken families, friends, and divided the community."

— *CBC News*, June 8, 2015

Therein lies the outports' predicament — the Government of Newfoundland *hates* outport people because communities accessible only by boat cost considerable money to service. So, because government values money more than anything else on earth, they're making life miserable for outport people.

I know — *hate* is a strong word, but I'm sticking with it, because the province knows exactly what they're doing. Newfoundland has resettled several hundred communities, so no one should be surprised that by increasing relocation money and insisting that people reach a ninety-percent agreement before accessing their offer, government is pitting neighbour against neighbour, even family against family, and that's despicable.

"Now what?" the majority of McCallum inquires. "Now that we know most of us want to go, but this is not good enough for government?" Their anguish goes on. "The school is [almost] empty, and children have no one to play with," say the 76 percent that are ready to roll but now have this enticing inertia-inducing cash-carrot dangling directly in front of their face.

"Our doctor doesn't come, people get older, and our weather, fishery, fish prices, ferry, [employment] insurance, drinking water . . . worse. Friends are not friends no more. Even families are fighting. People are depressed. And all we want to know," residents ask, "is if government can help this community get over this rotten mess? Because things are not going the way we need them to. No sir, after hundreds of years of people living in McCallum, things are not so good around here these days."

The ones who want to stay say a "government [report in the sixties] said that McCallum would not last, but here we are." But that's because many of those who were chased from communities like Mosquito and Muddy Hole relo-cated to McCallum. With no feeder-towns to facilitate such a resurgence today, it's difficult for even the most skillful rejectionist to argue that history is ripe to repeat itself.

Then there is the gang who have some really sweet rea-sons to stick around — the ones whose children and grand-children are still here. Lucky them. While drifters like me try our darnedest to define "home," this multi-generational crowd has figured out exactly where they want to live and die. It's probably not a coincidence, however, that several members of this McCallum-clinging team are in possession of some of the town's more rewarding employment posi-tions — there are not a lot of people pondering the possi-bility of voting in lieu of their own employment needs, and I'm a little surprised by this. I'm amazed that more folks don't vote to leave on the grounds that their friends and family wish to go, because these people seem so community-centred otherwise. I figure they're afraid that they won't be able to find comparable employment elsewhere. And, in a province where people are tremendously territorial, and institutions nepotistic, they're probably right.

Of course, there are others who are healthy, happy, and simply love the life so much that they don't want to part with it. In contrast, there are some with serious health issues who no longer have family around and are constantly dependent on someone else to assist, yet they consistently vote to stay, and this seems somewhat selfish to me. And then there are others who are afraid of the unknown — they are scared of what waits outside the outport.

This predicament isn't particularly pleasant for me either. There's a lot to not like about being part of a population where three out of four people wish they were someplace else. I've never been a fan of bad attitudes, and suddenly they're showing up in surprising places. Some people who seemed contented suddenly aren't. Plus, indecisiveness rules. Do we or don't we buy new windows for the church? What about boats, homes, boardwalks . . . ? This maintenance dilemma reaches far and wide, and it creeps into all conversations. With more and more of your neighbours leaving for the winter, your pipes are at greater risk than ever of freezing when flow is not adequate enough to keep them fluid. Even if you get up several times in the night to turn on your taps — a practice that greatly affects one's sleep, thus mood — there is no guarantee that you will have water in the morning. You can take my word on that. My home is at the end of a long, vulnerable line.

Plus, I'm lonely. I'm finding internet dating more difficult than I thought it would be. Five years in an isolated outport has been an incredible experience for me, but I'm tired of dreaming alone, and it would be nice to have someone to be intimate with once in a while. While I've done my best to work with this unpleasant situation, it doesn't dismiss the fact that I'm sad without someone to share it with.

Many on the mainland tell me that if they weren't married with children, they would do what I did — quit secure employment and take on a life of art and adventure — but they wouldn't. They're just fooling themselves. I'm not implying that children don't greatly affect choices. I'm pointing out that, with or without kids, freedom fighting is hard work. It takes a lot of psychological labour before a person can initiate large change in their life, and many people won't do weepy work. It's obvious, isn't it? When these parents blame their incapacity to initiate change on their partner and their children, not only is such a lack of accountability unconscionable, it's an indicator of these people's failure to see that having a partner and children could be — should be — their greatest adventure ever.

Even those who drag their feet can — if they truly want to — initiate enormous change once their gang has fled the nest. But I don't see that happening. From my perspective, post-retirement for the majority still looks like the life that came before it, just with a lot less employment, and a little more lawn care. The transition from job to retirement — however you define stepping down — can be extremely difficult. Yet we all have to face it eventually, unless we die young. So if you look at the changes I've made as being the same that my peers will ultimately confront — only ten years after I did — my actions stop seeming so out of the ordinary. We all have to decide what we want the last leg of our life to look like. Or, as one of my more sensitive and insightful McCallum buddies said after long and careful consideration, "Let me get this straight, old boy — you had a good job, and you were making big bucks and living on a beautiful farm in Ontario when, suddenly, you realized you wanted to be a Newfoundland lobster fisherman."

"That's right, my son," I teasingly tell him. "Except it wasn't so sudden. It took several years of emotional pain and suffering before my needs became even a tiny bit clear, and it was years after that before I could muster up the courage required to make such a jump. Even then I wasn't completely comfortable with my choices. I found lots of ways to self-sabotage . . . but, you're right, somewhere deep inside of me, I needed to sail the high seas."

What I didn't tell my buddy was my soul-searching process is ongoing. And that just as he was figuring this out about me, my world was changing once again.

I got an email this afternoon from a former love interest named Liz, informing me that she has recently removed herself and her kids from an extremely unhealthy household. Liz and I haven't communicated in fourteen years, yet there is no ambiguity in her inquiry — she wishes to know what the relationship part of my life presently looks like. I tell her I am alone in an isolated Newfoundland outport. My answer prompts her to ask a second question — she wants to know if I ever imagine myself returning to Ontario. I inform her of my plans, that I not that long ago decided my five-year Newfoundland adventure was coming to a close, and that returning to my home province is my intention.

Liz and her children have taken refuge in a women's shelter in Fenelon Falls — the town I coincidentally left for Newfoundland — where she is trying to decide their next move. You know how it is — you're in a major crisis, and you need room to be okay with that, but your desire to believe that everything is all right has you making an assortment of important decisions, even though you should be years away from that reality.

Liz is in no position to be determining anything and, to be fair, anyone in her situation is entitled to be in a decision-making mess for a long time afterwards. So she's desperately grasping for some semblance of stability, but there is none. There is only pain, and an ex-husband with a restraining order on his head. That's why women's shelters exist, so women can land on their feet after an enormous tragedy, and what better place to do that than around those suffering in similar circumstances, with a significant support system in place and all the modern security that today's technology can provide? In the meantime, Liz is clearly asking for my assistance, so I'm encouraging her to sit tight, catch her breath, and put herself and her children first. I tell her that I'll try from afar to fill in, where needed, but that she has to trust the process.

The hardest part for me is, I'm not free to go anywhere for a while. I'm currently committed to lobster fishing, and then I've got a lengthy string of friends and family visiting from Ontario after that. Plus, I've previously booked myself into Gampo Abbey — a Buddhist monastery in Cape Breton — where I intend to sit in silence for eight days. That means I'm not free to travel to Ontario for six months. Liz and I will have to find other ways to connect while she gets the professional help she needs and I tie up loose ends in Atlantic Canada.

So that's what we do. We exchange phone calls and emails with each other every day. While these forms of communication create opportunities for us to really get to know each other, it is difficult at times. I'm craving intimacy, and it's easy for me to see that I'm needed in Fenelon Falls. Guilt and shame are powerful forces, and Liz is clinging to them like barnacles to a boat. It's no secret that the majority of women who find themselves in the same hideous spot that Liz is in can feel a tremendous pull to return to the life that put them there in the first place. There is no doubt in my mind that I have to support her.

twenty-three

While 59 out of 76 residents said they wanted to leave McCallum, the 17 who opted to stay carried the day in the June 1 vote on possible relocation from the community . . . Linda Hennessey said she expects some people will leave regardless of the June 1 vote, which will make it harder for the 'Yes' side to ever receive the required 90 percent.

— Clayton Hunt, the *Carbonear Compass*, June 8, 2015

I've heard it said that after you've lived somewhere spectacular for a while, you start to take that place's gorgeousness for granted. This is not the case for me in McCallum. Many times every day, I look out at the dramatic cliffs and our almighty ocean and feel compelled to pinch myself and ask, "Do you know where you are, and have been for five years?"

My feelings for these outport people are also over the moon — I'm seriously attached to several of them. Same can be said for the culture. Lobster season is alive and thriving, and even though I find the work exhausting, I've never enjoyed a job more. What with Clyde's busted ribs, my load is a whole lot larger. It's nice to be needed, and the adventure that comes along with added responsibility has me in high spirits. On mornings like today when the fog's exceptionally thick, what's an already dodgy endeavour becomes even more dangerous. Especially after a full moon plays tricks with the tide, transforming what are normally deep, underwater rocks into big bombs sitting close to the surface.

If I'm asked to steer our boat out of the harbour — and no one with a brain would ever seriously consider such a suggestion — there's not a chance in the world that I could navigate the narrow channel we take out to the open ocean. I can't see ten feet in front of me. Fortunately, my skipper is unflappable. We've had some heavy rains and, given all the runoff, there is a risk of debris in the water, so Junior's got me on lookout for floaters — large logs, errant containers — something that could upset our boat should she come upon it quickly. We're travelling slowly while Junior cries out the names of landmarks that periodically barely appear on our right. "That's the Eye," he'll confidently call out, where all I can see is fractionally darker fog. A long time later he might shout, "Muddy Hole," "The Bird," or "Fish Head," and I'm not only surprised that he recognizes these hidden markers, but at how little distance we've travelled in the meantime.

I don't understand how travelling west along a foggy southern shoreline has to be so difficult — you just travel a close distance from what you can see on your right, right? But that's not accounting for sunkers and shag rocks. We'd be crazy to go anywhere near that rugged coastline. As it is, I have no idea how Junior missed running into Mosquito Island. I didn't even remember to watch for it until I realized he had intentionally pulled us up directly under its big, bold eastern end. And what about the lengthy openings that occur when we cross the mouth of a fiord, where there is *nothing* to be seen on the open sea? How Junior knows when, and how much, to turn our boat slightly southwest to accommodate the land change that awaits us at Dragon Bay is beyond me. It's as if my captain has a compass at his core. I appreciate his patience when I signal that there's something in the water to watch out for and it turns out to be nothing worth worrying about. "I'm just glad you got your eyes on," he is kind enough to say, while I swallow my pride and carry on.

I try to connect with the ghosts of those who travelled these waters before us, but today I'm finding that idea difficult. I feel disoriented in a lot of different ways. I'm unsure of where we are, my stomach is unexpectedly upset, and, while searching for spirits that previously belonged to courageous, hard-working fishing families, I find myself stumbling across lying selfish thieves who used this island to amass fortunes at the expense of others. Predatory merchants, deceitful politicians, and disgusting pirates like Peter Easton, who four hundred years ago worked these shores.

Sponsored by a scummy English family named Kelligrews, Easton moved to Newfoundland so he could be free to plunder without interference from the king. Then one winter he loaded two million pounds of gold onboard his boats and headed to the Azores Islands. It was in the Azores that Easton's wealth grew even greater. After stealing a Spanish treasure ship, he connected with corrupt Portuguese politicians who worked with him in ways that allowed them all to make massive fortunes on the backs of the less fortunate. Eventually settling in Italy, Easton retired as one of the world's wealthiest men.

Today I am imagining Easton at the helm of the *San Sebastien*. I'm picturing that lawless freebooter and his ignorant fleet, loaded with all the weaponry that dirty money can buy, approaching a single vessel belonging to men whose only wish was to safely return to Britain with enough income to feed their families. I tell Junior this, and he humours me with half a grin before he shakes his head in disbelief of my black magic.

Whatever witchcraft I turn to today, none of it is working. In fact, it feels like my attempts to access the supernatural are simply making me sicker. I notice that if I look inwards, my constitution feels terrible, but peering out into the fog isn't the answer either. I think that not being able to acquire a lengthy look at the land because of the foggy fortress that surrounds us is upsetting my biological and mental makeup. I need a long view of something stable if I hope to feel better, and today that's impossible to find. The fog is denying me the opportunity to get a glimpse of anything large, fixed, and steady. I'm left with nothing but the roll of the ocean. And I haven't a clue why this has to happen. Not that I think I'm some sort of big-shot fisherman who never feels queasy. Just that I have been out enough in bad weather that I'd begun to believe I had seasickness beat. Yet, nothing about anything is feeling good to me right now. My mind and body are rebelling. It starts like a migraine. A short time later, I sense a nauseous feeling. I don't immediately think I'm going to throw up, but my history tells me that what I am experiencing could easily escalate.

Junior is not surprised. He's knows a lot about life on the sea, and me. He knows I'm not normally so slow, nor is it my style to sit down so much. Junior figured out what was going on long before I did. "I wouldn't normally start in this area," he says as he expertly guides our craft into a large section of marauding water. "But they're calling for twelve- to fifteen-knot easterlies, so I want to pull these pots before things get too rough for you."

So that's what we do — we attend to the business at hand — but I must say that I'm not myself. The conversation I have in my head helps a little. This is all part of what you came to McCallum for — in for a penny, in for a pound, I remind myself. That puffiness around your eyes, the tightening of the muscles in your neck, and the terrible taste you sense in your throat every time you catch a whiff of the bait box? Forget about it. As for those huge gaping holes in the sea that open up every time the undertow sucks us towards sawtoothed rocks? Stop staring into them. Which I did. Until I couldn't anymore.

Vomiting is a violent event. The way the egg, toast, and oatmeal I had for breakfast come back up is not only scary, it's abusive to my body. It doesn't matter how often I've vomited, I still resist the next time, even when experience tells me that if I just allow myself to offload what's inside my stomach, I'll feel much better afterwards.

At least Junior finds it funny. "Don't vomit on our extra

lifejackets, Dave, when you crawl into the fetal position and start crying up under the bow," he says. "And don't think I'm taking you back in, you scurvy dog — I've used enough gas bringing your big body out here. There's no way I'm hauling you all the way back to McCallum without a full day's catch on board. And that's going to be hard to get, because the way you're throwing your breakfast overboard, those lobsters are not going to be bothering with our bait."

Vomit, spew, puke, gag, retch, hurl, or heave. Call it what you want. Only six more hours on increasingly rough seas, old man. But less time than that before some rotten fishermen we crossed paths with midmorning lets all of McCallum know that I barfed my breakfast overboard.

I call Claire Mowat at her Port Hope, Ontario, home. I ask what she's been up to. She informs me that she's been busy working with her accountant as they sort through everything that was, and still is, Farley Mowat Inc.

Claire and I have continued to occasionally correspond by snail mail — I send her postcards showing the Southwest at its best, and she writes me on an old-time typewriter. When Farley was still alive she told me that the two of them were reliving their Newfoundland lives vicariously through me. That was kind of her to say.

Claire's incredible. I still have a strong desire to connect with her, to share in our common Southwest Coast experience. I update her on the changing landscape called my love life, and I tell her that I think of this book that you're reading as a modern-day Farley Mowat. Then I suddenly feel insecure — there's been only one Farley — and I tell her so. She says, "There is nothing wrong with describing your book that way — you're saying it is an adventure story, a certain kind of genre, about a distinct way of life that my late husband played a big role in pioneering. There's nothing wrong with that."

Claire also answers my questions about Farley's passing. "Life certainly is different, learning to live alone after all these years," she says, "but I feel blessed that I had him for as long as I did. He was almost ninety-three, and he'd had a heart condition for fifteen years."

Aware of the Southwest's resettlement sadness, Claire offers up a desire of her own. "I hope Francois doesn't go," she states, and I know why. Aesthetically speaking, Francois is picture-perfect. "As for your book, I'll be the first to buy it," she adds. What a thrill that is for me to hear. When Farley Mowat's widow — a fine author in her own right

— states that she intends to be my book's first buyer, I tell myself that I'd better help to make that happen.

Claire's parents had a cottage in Fenelon Falls in the forties and fifties. "There was no one around at that time," she tells me. "They had miles of shoreline along the Burnt River all to themselves."

Claire remembers Fenelon Falls fondly. When I tell her that I am struggling with the idea of living there — of returning to a place I swore I never would — she once again shows me what a caring, calming influence she can be. "There is nothing like a small town," she reminds me. Then, when it comes time to sign off, she insists that I "enjoy Fenelon Falls," in a way that tells me I need to get on with whatever's ahead. In a world where I am often asked to help others sort through their thoughts and dreams, it's sweet how generously Claire performs this act for me.

twenty-four

Hennessey is not hopeful the town will ever get the required 90 per cent, but says she will continue to fight for relocation for as long as she can.

— Laura Howells, CBC News, June 8, 2015

I think that freedom — the ability to act as one wants — whether you measure it with time, money, talent, flexibility, or other forms of currency, can only be fully realized by leveraging that liberty. All the money in the world, for example, is worthless if you don't use it in ways that work. Not that I don't recognize the comfort that comes with having a reservoir of resources. Just that I think that dying with a lot of money (or unused flexibility, or unrealized talent, or . . .) in the bank would be, for me, a disastrous way to go out. So after sitting, single, for five years in an isolated outport, with an excess of freedom at my fingertips, I believe that I should know by now what I'm willing to spend it on, and I do. I'm ready to leverage it on Liz.

I feel like I've spent my entire adult life preparing for what is, admittedly, an unsettling circumstance — I'm considering giving my heart to one seriously messed up mother of two with a scary past and a dangerously dysfunctional day-to-day — and that if I'm not emotionally strong enough to work with Liz's pain by now, I never will be. I still have a lot of personal issues of my own, but I'm convinced that I'm in a capable place when it comes to controlling them. So if I find that I'm overwhelmed with the seriousness of Liz's situation — she's full of fear, and her primary coping mechanism is denial — I've got no one to blame but myself. In the meantime, Liz looks like my adventure of a lifetime.

So I lean a broom against the door to my little McCallum house. A broom across your door, in McCallum, is a way of telling others that no one is home. That broom says, "If you're needing something inside, you'll have to help yourself." Then I slide down the stairs that Lloyd Durnford built for me after my old ones rotted away.

My walk to the wharf is not a private one. Everybody sees me leaving and asks where I'm going. The funniest part of this pattern is almost everyone knows my answers in advance. Word of mouth in McCallum moves more quickly than any of us let on. I'm not complaining. A lot of people are only wanting to make small talk. Asking where you're going, and for how long, is not a lot different than conversing about the weather. Or it was before resettlement money was offered. Now the thought of someone leaving strikes deep at the core of our basic fear that we may end up alone and lonely.

I'm not only talking about the people who want to leave McCallum but feel they can't. The gang that votes to stay also doesn't want anyone to leave. They might pretend that they've been too busy to think about such thoughts, but the most common dream that most outport people wish for is the one where things go back to the way they were when they were young. And that fantasy works best when everyone is present.

This feeling of dread regarding utter abandonment is not unique to outports, of course. It's just more obvious in this fishbowl environment, how we struggle with change. In McCallum, this dilemma is in your face every day when people's eyes well up with tears at talk of days gone by.

I remember when a National Geographic photographer from France visited McCallum. I showed him Farley Mowat's old book, *This Rock within the Sea*, which contains photographs of outport people in the sixties, living their lives along the Southwest Coast. Those photographs, taken by John de Visser of Cobourg, Ontario, show outport people inside their homes, partying, praying, posing . . . There is even a series of photos taken at a funeral, something I would never attempt to do today for fear of offending.

My new National Geographic photographer friend and I tried to figure out why it is that de Visser, who only visited the region for a brief time, had so much more freedom to document outport people living their private lives than photographers do today. I said it was because those with the pluck to pose for a photo have moved onto the likes of Ontario, Boston, or Alberta. There are personal reasons that a particular profile of person remains in McCallum — they're genuinely private, and often shy.

My friend thought that when de Visser snapped his photographs, people were not as aware of the way that images can be used abusively — that there weren't as many photos travelling the world for the sole purpose of humiliating those pictured in them. I think that when Farley Mowat brought international attention to Burgeo's cringeworthy whale killing, the Southwest Coast got its first taste of this public shaming way of life, and that everyone today is extremely aware of how technology has increased the potential for big-time embarrassment.

There also aren't as many people living on the Southwest Coast as there were when Mowat and de Visser visited. There aren't even as many as there were when *I* arrived. Where my McCallum home sits today stand three empty houses that only five years ago contained a total of ten residents. The house closest to that cluster is also no longer occupied, since McCallum's oldest person passed away.

Reginald James Fudge was a sweetheart. He was always friendly to my out-of-province visitors. Perhaps his experiences on Halifax fishing boats helped him adjust to the idea of interacting with outsiders. But whatever his motivation, Reg always found time to say hello or talk hockey with my company as they came and went.

Reg watched a lot of hockey. More than five hundred games per year, what with today's satellite access. It's no wonder Reg did so well in McCallum's weekly hockey pool. "The night after the Leafs made their trades, I watched to see how the new players was doing," he once told me. "I watched the Calgary game first, and then I watched the Anaheim game [an 11:30 p.m. start in Newfoundland]. The guys the Leafs got did good, but the guys they traded did not . . . No, my son, the boys who went to Calgary didn't do so good."

Reg found hockey to be "a good way to pass the time," and with his home sitting at the bottom of a steep granite cliff that blocked sunlight from reaching him for six months of the year, passing time was no small consideration. "I'd like to be outside, chopping wood, or helping my sons, but I can't no more," he'd say, in reference to his declining body. "So I watch a lot of hockey."

Reg and I would occasionally talk about a time when McCallum had no televisions. "I remember when Canada beat Russia — the game when Henderson scored in the last minute," he'd say. "We took a radio on the boat so we could listen while we pulled in nets.

"And I remember listening to a game between Montreal and Boston — Boston was winning 6–1, but Montreal won the game." While Reg's recollection of that contest was fun to hear, it's the hearty way in which he laughed at that memory that stuck with me. A Boston fan, Reg's tendency to laugh at a Bruins loss served to illustrate one of his most appealing qualities — Reg took neither the game nor himself too seriously.

Even when his body no longer cooperated, the way that Reg moved on his long walk to and from church was more graceful than most men. I don't know how he did it. I remember another time when he handed me a huge bag of scallops — each one as big as a golf ball — when I knew how hard it must have been for him to help pull the cage those critters were caught in off the ocean floor and into the boat. It was easy to see that Reg once lived a very different life, raising six children with his late wife Annie, fishing and hunting, picking berries, and going in the country for weeks at a time without cell phones, fibreglass boats, and heavily horse-powered motors.

I was proud to be part of the team that buried Reg. While others faced the strenuous job of digging, picking, and jackhammering through granite, I was asked to assist with the careful lowering of the casket, and the backfilling of the hole. I saw those tasks as my final chance to assist with anything Uncle Reg–related. Even when staring down death, Reg was considerate. He sent a last-minute message to the burial crew, telling them that he knew how difficult jackhammering through rock can be, so no one was to worry about the depth of his grave. "I'll be all right, my son," he said.

Reg's son Herman — McCallum's unofficial greeter — had to leave town as a result of his dad's death, what with no one to take care of him. While saddened by his father's passing, Herman took his own departure well. Herman saw himself as leaving on a great adventure. He stood at the starboard waving, smiling, and parroting messages he had heard others express about the sad state of affairs in McCallum, as the ferry pulled away from the wharf. Herman's leaving, however, left a large hole in McCallum's heart, because Herman brought more volume, energy, and identity to this community than the rest of us put together.

Tim Fudge — Reg's highly capable late-thirties son who was left alone at home after Herman moved on — was forced to relocate as well, but only to another McCallum locale, after his water froze when there were no longer enough neighbours nearby to facilitate adequate flow. It had been Reg's job to keep that water moving and their wood stove stoked while Tim went out to work. Tim said that when he finally left the family home, he felt like he was leaving his dear old dad behind, so he went back and plugged in nightlights. Such a sweet and thoughtful thing to do, and so symbolic of all that's right around here. Yet the vocal majority in this beleaguered province, and politicians as a whole, insist on treating these outport people poorly.

Everything dies, even communities and multigenerational ways of life — I realize that — but in the meantime, we don't need to rob these dying entities of their dignity.

This province can support these few people with something other than cold, hard, unconfirmed cash and contempt. Civil servants could work with outport people regarding their situation and include them in the planning process. The Southwest Coast might be a difficult place to call home these days, but it doesn't have to be nearly as hard as it is. If only the empowered could be compassionate — a concept completely lost on Newfoundland leadership.

The next part of my walk is an undisputedly desolate stretch. The Pooles have gone to Gander, where Ivy's need for dialysis can be best addressed, the Fudges have left for St. John's, where they can better deal with Elsie's Alzheimer's, and the Crants are visiting their children in Montreal. On those rare occasions where I encounter someone walking the other way, it's not uncommon for talk to be about resettlement. When I speak with those who wish to take the money, their resentment is greater than ever, while those who chose to stay will say, "Thank God all those hard feelings are gone, and things are back to normal."

People often ask me how I vote regarding resettlement. I tell them that I consider three points of personal importance. One: if I was motivated by money, I would have stayed in Ontario. Two: I didn't come here to tell twelfth-generation fishing families how to live their lives. And three: a quarter of a million dollars is a lot of money, so I owe it to myself to consider government's offer very carefully.

No doubt my final point causes the majority to believe that I vote to leave, but what they don't realize is, if I had been born and raised on the Southwest Coast, I would be in one of two camps — long gone or here until death, as long as no one had to excessively look after me in the meantime.

Yet I don't blame the ones who wish to go. They're getting older and need more medical attention, and almost all of those they care about are gone. Plus, *it's time* — people have reached a point where they are finally good with going. I'm thrilled for them for that. So I waffle back and forth regarding this resettlement thing, because at the end of the day, I believe that everybody is entitled to a vote. It's not the fault of anyone around here that the province of Newfoundland has such a hurtful way of doing business.

As I walk my final steps, I run out of time to talk. While this ferry's crew would never intentionally leave without me, they do have a schedule to keep. This gives me an excuse to slip quickly past the post office, an endless but emotional source of everyday pleasure for me over the past five years, given the friendship I share with the two beautiful women who have managed it throughout my time here. Another place of friendship, Fudge's Store, is right next door. Fudge's has been good to me as well, although never so intimate as a quiet little post office in an isolated outport. That opportunity to occasionally talk privately with Linda Durnford or Sharon Feaver has been one of my life's greatest gifts.

I note that Norman Durnford's home is also empty. Norm has got himself a Sandyville apartment but is finding it hard to stay away from McCallum most days. And I see that Clyde Feaver is waiting on the wharf, an occurrence that I'm convinced is more than coincidence. I believe my guardian angels have sent Clyde to say goodbye on behalf of the Feaver family, so I quietly acknowledge his princely presence before I board that big rusty boat. "Have a good trip," he tells me, as I do my best to address him directly.

The boys crank in the catwalk as I stroll to the stern. I know all too well that the back of this boat will be the best place for me to watch McCallum vanish into the fog. Everyone but Lloyd and Linda — my confidantes — have been told that I'm leaving to do some Cape Breton camping, but the truth is, after partaking in my eight-day meditation retreat, I'll be travelling to Fenelon Falls. I've got an Ontario beauty who needs my assistance, and, in complicated ways that I don't fully understand, I need her help as well.

I spoke with Sarah Fudge on the phone today. She and her husband, Matt, have moved into a basement apartment in their son's St. John's home. Sarah is the woman you were introduced to at the start of this story — the aunt who helped Herman with his Christmas card collection.

Herman's now in Pool's Cove, a Fortune Bay community of two hundred people, where he is living happily ever after with friends of the Fudges'. "Herman *had* to leave McCallum — he could not have stayed," Sarah insists. "There is no longer anyone in McCallum who could take care of him. He used to drop by everybody's house in the evening, and he would no longer have enough people to visit with, or feed him, if he was still there.

"McCallum is lonely these days. There were less than fifty people there last Christmas. Except for Clyde and Flora, and Howard and Maisy, there is no longer anybody living on the hill. Hartland and Lillian are in Lewisporte, where they can be closer to their son. And Tim has moved into George Blake's old house — he has done it up cute as a button — so after you go past Jason and April's home, there is nobody living on the point, either."

The always-thinking Sarah soon returns to talking about her St. John's situation. "Matt's happy here," she says. "Who would have thought that? But I can't say that I don't miss my old house. If our son Reguel had not died, I would have stayed in McCallum to take care of him. But Reguel's *not* in McCallum, so I'm happy here. We've got a beautiful apartment, with new paint and drywall. Tracy visits all the time, Michael comes in some days for his job too. The only child I didn't see last Christmas was Alvin in Deer Lake.

"So listen, my dear, because there are two things I want to tell you. The first one is, don't get me wrong, McCallum will always be my home, but there is no longer any reason for Matt and I to live there. And the second thing I want to say is, wherever you go, I hope you always remember how much we love you."

Same to you, Sarah. Yes, my dear — same to you all.